Captive No More ___ multitudes because it was writt___ ___ ___ woman of God who lived as a captive for y___ ___inking God had left her, she struggled until she found out that God is a God of love who doesn't punish his children but wants them to have the very best in life. Releasing her fears and anxieties, Tina began to overcome, and now she is able to help and comfort those who are going through the same thing. She is an imitator of the Lord Jesus and is full of love and compassion.

—Dodie Osteen, co-founder
of Lakewood Church

In *Captive No More*, Tina Underwood brings clarity to our hearts as she helps us face the fears, insecurities, and rejections we have all experienced in life. Tina gives deep insight into the grace of God and how this grace brings healing, deliverance, wholeness, and abundance to our lives. I am confident that this book will unlock the chains that have kept many in the body of Christ in bondage and away from the fullness of the life God always intended for us to enjoy. I invite you to dive deeply into its pages so you can step out into freedom.

—Joan E. Murray, author,
Called and Chosen for Destiny

Whether you're a new believer or one who's known the Lord a long time, you will find insights in *Captive No More* that will take you through the essential process of learning who you are in Christ. Tina's use of Scripture, revelation of its practical application, and the sharing of her personal journey combine to give us real help, hope, and assurance that we can indeed be captive no more.

—Peggy Gerst, president,
Strategic Ministries Inc.

Tina Underwood is one of the most powerfully anointed teachers and ministers I know in the area of inner healing. *Captive No More* skillfully tackles stumbling blocks we all face, like doubt, un-forgiveness, and rejection, and is a must-read for anyone desiring to reach his full potential in Christ.

—Steve Austin, director, Pastoral
Care Ministries, Lakewood Church

Many people spend years of counseling and therapy to overcome the hurt and pain of their past. Tina knew that only God could heal the pains of her past, and she took bold steps to put God's Word into action in her own life. It was through her own search for healing and wholeness that gave birth to *Captive No More*. I believe that God will use *Captive No More* to help people at every stage in life gain a deeper understanding of God's forgiveness, unconditional love, and healing power. The biblical truths and revolutionary principles found in this book will help everyone find ultimate freedom that only Jesus can give. Today is your day to be captive no more!

—Duncan Dodds, executive director,
Joel Osteen Ministries & Lakewood Church

CAPTIVE

Getting Over You So You Can Go On With God

NO MORE

TINA UNDERWOOD

CAPTIVE

Getting Over You So You Can Go On With God

NO MORE

TATE PUBLISHING & Enterprises

Captive No More
Copyright © 2009 by Tina Underwood. All rights reserved.

No part of this publication may be reproduced, stored in a retrieval system or transmitted in any way by any means, electronic, mechanical, photocopy, recording or otherwise without the prior permission of the author except as provided by USA copyright law.

Scripture quotations marked (AMP) are taken from the *Amplified Bible,* Copyright © 1954, 1958, 1962, 1964, 1965, 1987 by The Lockman Foundation. Used by permission.

Scripture quotations marked (KJV) are taken from the *Holy Bible, King James Version,* Cambridge, 1769. Used by permission. All rights reserved.

Scripture quotations marked (MSG) are taken from *The Message.* Copyright © 1993, 1994, 1995, 1996, 2000, 2001, 2002. Used by permission of NavPress Publishing Group.

Scripture quotations marked (NASB) are taken from the *New American Standard Bible®,* Copyright © 1960, 1962, 1963, 1968, 1971, 1972, 1973, 1975, 1977, 1995 by The Lockman Foundation. Used by permission.

Scripture quotations marked (NIV) are taken from the *Holy Bible, New International Version®.* NIV®. Copyright© 1973, 1978, 1984 by International Bible Society. Used by permission of Zondervan. All rights reserved.

Scripture quotations marked (NLT) are taken from the *Holy Bible, New Living Translation,* copyright © 1996. Used by permission of Tyndale House Publishers, Inc., Wheaton, Illinois 60189. All rights reserved.

The opinions expressed by the author are not necessarily those of Tate Publishing, LLC.

Published by Tate Publishing & Enterprises, LLC
127 E. Trade Center Terrace | Mustang, Oklahoma 73064 USA
1.888.361.9473 | www.tatepublishing.com

Tate Publishing is committed to excellence in the publishing industry. The company reflects the philosophy established by the founders, based on Psalm 68:11,
"The Lord gave the word and great was the company of those who published it."

Book design copyright © 2009 by Tate Publishing, LLC. All rights reserved.
Cover design by Kellie Southerland
Interior design by Stefanie Rooney

Published in the United States of America

ISBN: 978-1-61566-480-1
1. Religion, Christian Life, Personal Growth
2. Religion, Christian Life, Spiritual Growth
09.11.16

Dedication

This book is dedicated to God as Father, Son, and Holy Spirit. Everything I've learned has been because of your goodness and mercy. Your power to take a broken soul, save it, love it, and put it back together is beyond anything I could ask or think. I'm forever grateful and in your service.

Acknowledgments

Nothing in this life is achieved alone; therefore, my deepest thanks to every person who has invested his or her time in this work. There are more teachers, mentors, friends, and loved ones that I can count, but to each one of you, I am forever grateful.

A special thanks:

To my husband, Lance. Your genuine love, unwavering support, and kind friendship have made it possible for me to bloom.

To my boys, Jeremy and Neal, for giving me a reason (you two) for wanting to be a better me.

To my girls, Jaclyn and Lindsay. I'm so grateful that you are part of our family.

To Grace and Dean. Who knew I could love you so much!

To my sister, Nancy Franklin. You have walked through life with me (the good, the bad, and the ugly), all the while being my biggest cheerleader. You rock!

To every person and friend who worked on this project, especially Michelle Flippin, Valencia Anderson, Julia Rigos, Sarah Mathai, and Dora Pezzotti. I couldn't have done this without you.

To my dear friends Lyn Fitzpatrick, Charrisa Aripe, and Eliana Reinsvold, thanks for loving me and keeping me real.

To Joan Murray of Joan Murray Ministries, thank you for your prayers, support, and friendship. You have shared your journey so selflessly!

To my friend Duncan Dodds. You showed me that there could be more!

Table of Contents

Foreword

"Christ has set us free to live a free life. So take your stand! Never again let anyone put a harness of slavery on you" (Galatians 5:1, MSG).

I couldn't agree more with Tina Underwood's passionate call for the body of Christ to embrace both the gift and challenge of entering into a deeper experience of the healing and freedom Jesus secured for us who believe.

Within the pages of *Captive No More,* I came face to face with the passion and love for the body of Christ which dwell authentically within Tina and compel her to open wide her heart to pen these encouraging words. Tina charts a hope-filled path for others to follow that originates with her personal encounters and experiences with the liberating truths and life principles you will find between the covers of this valiant call to wholeness.

The truth is clear: our personal wholeness and the health of our relationships will either validate or discount our proclamation of the good news of humanity's rescue through Jesus Christ. Before the body of Christ can come close to fulfilling its mandate of discipling the nations and proclaiming the ultimate setting-right of all things, it will need to embody more of what this God of ours looks like. Proclamation without demonstration, unfortunately, has significantly contributed to the distorted images of our heavenly Father embraced by many of our neighbors, friends, and even entire cultures. We must never allow the Great Commission to eclipse the great commandment from which our true identity and all our strength, growth, and creative energies originate.

Captive No More is a message of hope, a clear call to believe and trust in God's goodness and love for each one of us. Within these pages is also a strong admonition for the body of Christ to grow up and "move out," to take possession of and settle into our promised freedom: our inheritance in Christ Jesus. Someone once stated, "You'll never know the depths to which you have fallen until you start the climb back." For those looking for companionship and wisdom on their spiritual journey, you are sure to discover the life-giving truth and assurance that you are not alone.

The truth is (because you are holding this book in your hands), that God is already at work in you. If you are desiring more of the promised "abundant life," longing for greater contentment, peace, and joy, wanting to deepen your relationships, or maybe just sick and tired of being sick and tired, recognize these are all precious gifts, the very cords of love by which the Father is drawing you toward healing and wholeness. Allow this awareness to draw you into God's love and care and stand your ground against the tempter's lies to settle for anything less than God's glory and purpose for you.

Listen to the Healer's voice in these pages encouraging and empowering you to be honest with your pain, humble in the grace of acknowledging your inability to heal yourself, and hopeful in God's promise to bring you into the light and truth that will set you amazingly free!

The apostle Paul stated confidently, "And I am certain that God, who began the good work within you, will continue his work until it is finally finished on the day when Christ Jesus returns" (Philippians 1:6, NLT). Give yourself permission to believe that your heavenly Father really does have your best interests in mind, that he has the power to restore righteousness, peace, and joy to you, and that he delights in making you flourish.

Take this journey as I have done and experience God's custom-fit grace and the enduring freedom of being *Captive No More.*

—Michael Green, associate pastor,
Calvary Community Church, Houston, Texas

Introduction

Do you feel that church, Christianity, and even God have let you down? Are you tired of trying to believe for good, only to be disappointed again? Maybe it seems things will never change, and your heart is broken over years of trying and failing in this walk of life. If so, I have some good news!

It's time to look at things honestly, getting rid of beliefs about God that have caused life to be anything but good. After years of helping others overcome their hurts and strongholds, I've found some common issues in the lives of God's people. These issues of disappointment, frustration, and hopelessness, causing guilt and condemnation in our hearts, are directed toward God because of a lack of knowledge. We incorrectly blame God for letting us down, and by doing so, set ourselves up for more disappointment.

After years of believing that I had somehow been left out of the good-life circle, I discovered that God had not let me down and that he was neither punishing me nor keeping me from good. I grew up believing that every bad thing that happened was God punishing me in some way. I spent years trying to figure out what had made me so bad that he had to keep causing me pain. Although I always had a sense of God's presence in my life through all of the hurt and disappointment, I determined at a young age that he was not doing a very good job of being God, so it was my responsibility to carry my world on my shoulders. I also asked those same hurting questions that many have asked me, such as, *Where was God when I needed him?*

Let me assure you that what I've learned over the last twenty-seven years of walking with God is that he is not the variable; he does not let us down. God is good! He really is good all of the time, but we've complicated things by trying to fit God into our molds. With our finite minds, we conclude that we must be inherently unlovable for all the hurts and disappointments to continue happening. Because of our wrong beliefs, we settle for far less than God intended. The truth is, God really does love us, each and every one of us, and has a great plan for our lives. When we come to the knowledge of his love, we can begin to walk out the real plan that God intended and which Jesus died to give us.

Captive No More is a culmination of the truths the Lord used to set me free from all the lies and pain that kept me in bondage. These truths have helped many find the ability to live in freedom. To be really free, I had to do it his way, and his way is spelled out in John 8:32 (NKJV): "You will know the truth, and the truth shall make you free." I have concluded, after years of helping people overcome their past that there is one universal answer to our problem, and that is, we must know the truth of God's love for ourselves. How many of us have simply accepted the negative things in our lives as *just the way it is,* not willing to face the chance of disappointment or defeat? It is time to lay down all the excuses that have caused us to stay in the place of mediocrity. It's time to get to the truth of the love of God and how he sees us. You see, I believe that we have a responsibility on this earth to know God, to believe his love, and then to share that love with others.

Freedom requires something from us. It requires us taking responsibility for ourselves and for the things we need to change but ultimately learning to trust our hearts and lives into the Father's capable hands.

As you go through these pages with me, you will see the traps that have bound you and find the answers to those traps. I promise that if you take these truths and apply them, you will find your heart beginning to heal. My prayer is that you come to know how precious you are to the Father, and by knowing that truth, you will become *Captive No More.*

A Firm Foundation

During my years in ministry, I have heard countless stories of lives broken and bruised by the lingering devastation of horrific circumstances such as physical, emotional, and sexual abuse. Other life-altering situations such as divorce, loss, sickness, and pain have proven to cause just as much destruction to one's sense of self and well-being. While life can and will always throw unexpected twists and turns, I would venture to say that some of the deepest and most extreme wounds often come at the hands of those closest to us, namely, our family and trusted friends.

Personally, I believe that there is no devastation or betrayal that can rival such pain received at the hand of a family member or trusted friend. This pain knows no bounds, and while we common folk have all tasted bitter grapes, even celebrity status cannot insulate a person from its cruel effects. The psalmist and noteworthy King David expressed something that many of us can identify with when he said, "Yea, mine own familiar friend, in whom I trusted, which did eat of my bread, hath lifted up his heel against me" (Psalm 41:9 KJV). Can you hear his pain and confusion? I don't know about you, but as I read it, I almost feel a tangible sting. In layman's terms, the renowned leader whose praises and great exploits are still sung experienced the shocking reality that he too could be betrayed.

God's Compassion

I am often astounded at how we, mere humans, have the capacity to survive such pain, and while we possess this remarkable capability to bear up under the most pressing circumstances, what I find totally awesome is God's compassion for the brokenhearted. It literally surpasses anything we ever experience in our earthly relationships. Unquestionably, it is his immeasurable love for us that causes the God of the entire creation to take careful note of the individual pains we endure in our human experience. These wounds have not gone unnoticed.

Psalm 56:8 says that God keeps track of our sorrow and collects our tears in a bottle. In other words, to God, there are no insignificant hurts. Each disappointment and betrayal affects him and garners deep understanding, help, and support. What a testament to his thoughts toward us! Friend, he has our healing and restoration in mind. Moreover, there is a deliverance that awaits us. The question that I pose today is this: Are you ready to be delivered? To be truly set free?

Many of us say that we want to be set free, but rarely do we consider the fact that God's desire for our healing far exceeds that of our own. Tenderly and patiently, our Father works beneath the surface to uncover the abscesses in our lives. We know the ones—those putrid, festering wounds that we quickly tend to with remedies of our own. Rather than taking the time required for a total and complete healing, we look for quick and temporary fixes, never really healed, just well enough to get by, barely strong enough to cope.

God never promised us a life where we settle for just getting by or just coping. That kind of pseudo-existence is not reflective of the *zoë* life (the God kind of super-abundant life) Christ died to purchase for us. If we take the premise that we can continue to coexist with our wounds while still exuding some semblance of productivity, the wound will one day transform into a stronghold. Unbeknownst to us, that quietly growing stronghold will slowly take hold of our personalities and eventually hinder us from fulfilling our destinies.

Strongholds

We form strongholds in our minds when we do not know how to deal correctly with the pain and disappointments we face in life. Any time we try to meet legitimate needs (e.g., the need for love, acceptance, or protection) in illegitimate ways, we have a propensity to build a stronghold. By definition, a stronghold is described as a fortification or place of security. Practically speaking, strongholds are defense mechanisms we employ to protect ourselves from pain. Although response to pain can be similar, each person is unique and therefore adds a unique layer to the rapidly multiplying strongholds that exist. *How many strongholds exist?* we ask. Untold hundreds. Bitterness, pride, doubt, rejection, and fear are just a few examples. As mentioned earlier, strongholds can form in many ways because no two people handle pain the same. Most strongholds form early in life, when we are children and therefore more vulnerable to pain. Being so young, we haven't yet developed the skill or emotional muscles to understand how to process pain correctly, and as the years progressed, life taught us that if we erect a wall of bitterness and strife between us and our perceived enemy, this construction will insulate us from future hurt.

This couldn't be further from the truth. What's more, even our suspicions and doubts are a form of protection, albeit faulty, that temporarily shield us from additional disappointment. No matter how secure you might feel in the shelter of those walls, you must remember that every stronghold is built upon a lie. These strongholds form false walls of protection around our souls, but be warned, the diabolical truth about a stronghold is that while it does a good job at walling us in, this same stronghold also walls everyone else out. Make no mistake about it; strongholds imprison us. We become captive to our own ways and methods, making it extremely difficult for us to see any other way of dealing with pain.

Your Foundation

Everyone has a base system of beliefs, or what I would call a *foundation.* Our foundations start to form early in life and are largely shaped by our childhood experiences and environments. Due to faulty teaching or a lack of teaching altogether, these foundations can be cracked, broken, or improperly placed, and each time we choose to believe lies, new cracks occur. Every person has a foundation upon which he or she continues to build, whether it is true or false. This is the foundation upon which he or she will build for the duration of his or her life. As we can imagine, it is difficult to stand steady or walk a straight and narrow road when the ground beneath our feet is faltering. Anything that is built upon a cracked foundation will not stand.

Would you allow me to tell you some good news? I mean some really good news. Jesus Christ is the only sure foundation. "For no other foundation can anyone lay than that which is [already] laid, which is Jesus Christ (the Messiah, the Anointed One)" (1 Corinthians 3:11 AMP).

Ephesians 3:17–19 instructs us to be rooted deep and founded securely on love. God is love. Jude verse 20 in the Amplified Bible instructs us to "build ourselves up [founded] on our most holy faith [make progress, rise like an edifice higher and higher]."

Our foundations reflect what we believe about God and ourselves and thereby determine the outcome and quality of our lives. If we have firm foundations, we are more likely to live the abundant lives that Christ died to give us, but if we have faulty foundations, the worries of this world can easily trip us up. No matter how hard we try, we will not produce what God intended as long as we are building on faulty foundations. We will not attain the healing and the wholeness God desires for us if we do not truly know who God is, or who we are in Christ.

When I stepped out to fulfill my calling as a minister of the Word, I was not standing on solid ground. I did not know who I was in Christ or what I meant to God. My worth and identity were based on what I did rather than what Christ had done for me. I cared more about what other people thought of me than what God thought of me. I was still trying to protect myself.

Repairing the Foundation

Little did I know that God had a great plan for my healing and deliverance. The master architect and engineer designed a new blueprint for my foundation. Thankfully, that old foundation didn't have to be completely wiped away. God rebuilt the ruins of my life and raised up the foundation that had long been devastated. Best of all, I was able to keep living while the work was being done. God handed me a road map for the long journey ahead and graciously sent workers to help me along the way.

A perfect illustration of God's beautification process to bring his children to a place of restoration and wholeness is evidenced in the diligent care and attention my husband, Lance, took to repair our broken walkway. Lance carefully removed and repaired one brick at a time. During the process, the walkway was always passable, but it wasn't complete. He took the time required to make a slipshod surface into one that not only supports those who use it but is also lovely to behold. Similarly, the truth of God's Word exposes and fills the cracks in our foundations little by little. We do not have to stop living while God is restoring the damage. We can still go to work, take care of our children, and continue on our journey. And get this: God can fix our foundations while we are standing on them. Now, that's amazing grace!

While we cannot fix the weak spots in our foundations, we can trust God to fix them for us. Instead of focusing on our faults, we should fix our eyes on Christ. What you focus on will grow, so the choice is yours. Do you want to magnify your weaknesses or the one whose power is made perfect in your weakness? "[Not in your own strength] for it is God who is all the while effectually at work in you [energizing and creating in you the power and desire], both to will and to work for His good pleasure and satisfaction and delight" (Philippians 2:13 AMP). However, we will not tap into the power of God if we do not know him and what he offers.

We have to know God for ourselves. *Yada,* the Hebrew word for *know,* means to intimately and progressively come to know the Lord. The only way we can do this is by spending time with him. In order to come to know him, we must be willing to take the critical first step, and that is to enter into a personal relationship with Jesus Christ. As we spend time with the Lord in prayer and in his Word, our relationship will grow. Then, as our relationship develops, we begin to see and understand the importance of obedience in building a strong foundation. When we come to know and live by God's Word, we are not easily moved by the storms of life.

> For everyone who comes to Me and listens to My words [in order to heed their teaching] and does them, I will show you what he is like: He is like a man building a house, who dug and went down deep and laid a foundation upon the rock; and when a flood arose, the torrent broke against that house and could not shake or move it, because it had been securely built or founded on a rock. But he who merely hears and does not practice doing My words is like a man who built a house on the ground without a foundation, against which the torrent burst, and immediately it collapsed and fell, and the breaking and ruin of that house was great.
>
> Luke 6:47–49 (AMP)

I have ministered to many people over the years who have wasted a lot of time and energy trying to fix their own weaknesses. Their efforts were ineffective because they were leaning upon themselves rather than upon God. "Unless the Lord builds the house, its builders labor in vain" (Psalm 127:1 NIV). Make no mistake about it; anything we try to do apart from God will not succeed. Our efforts at being better Christians will not benefit us if our core beliefs about God are not correct. It is better to spend our time getting to know the Lord than it is trying to work out our issues. We will experience much more success, even by accident, with a firm foundation than we ever would on purpose operating from a faulty one. It is better to let God love us than try to fix ourselves. Having a firm foundation of truth will make us holier than our works ever will. As ministers, we can try to teach Christians to be righteous, sanctified, and holy, but if fear is their motivation, they will not stand firm in righteousness and holiness. Only when our actions are motivated by God's love can we remain blameless and pure.

John 3:16 tells us that God so loved the world that he sent his one and only Son to die for us so that we might have eternal life. God paid a high price—the life of his Son—so that we could be in right relationship with him. Christ took the punishment we deserved and gave us his righteousness instead. Many people have faith to believe and accept God's gift of salvation; however, few in the body of Christ enjoy the fullness of their salvation, which includes healing, deliverance, and wholeness.

Isaiah 61:1 says that Jesus came to set the captives free. Through his sacrifice on the cross, we have been redeemed, bought out of the slavery of bondage and captivity; we have been ransomed and do not have to pay our own way. The freedom Christ died to give us has been paid for in full. Although freedom is already ours in Christ, we have to learn how to appropriate that freedom in our daily lives. To appropriate means to *own for oneself.* We own our freedom as we come to know and believe who we are in Christ. It is not enough just to hear the truth of God's Word; we have to learn how to apply that truth to our lives. When the truth resonates in our hearts, we are set free from bondage.

> My people are destroyed for lack of knowledge.
>
> Hosea 4:6 (KJV)

It is not God's will that any man should perish; rather, it is his desire that all people walk in physical, mental, emotional, and spiritual health. God's divine healing is already ours. Isaiah 53:5 (AMP) says, "With the stripes [that wounded] Him we are healed and made whole." Our job is to pull what Christ has done for us into the here and now, into our present reality, and the way we do this is by faith. God answers every prayer that we pray in faith. God heals us where our faith is, but some people don't know they can believe for emotional healing. God is not mad at us for not knowing; however, he wants us to know the truth so that we do not perish. He wants us to experience the fullness of our salvation.

Our whole foundation is built on the image we have of God. We need to make sure that the image we have of both God and ourselves lines up with the truth of the Word of God. If either image is skewed, we will believe lies instead of the truth. Let's take a moment and consider the following: Can we identify what has tarnished our image of God and ourselves? What lies have we believed? These lies have to be kicked out in order to make room for the truth because we will never see either God or ourselves correctly until we know and believe the truth.

We all have angels assigned to us, and I often wonder what they must think when they see us, the redeemed of the Lord, struggling along in our own strength. I can almost hear their questions. *Why is that woman's head down? Why is that man not excited about what God is doing in his life? Do God's children not have a clue about who they are?*

If we are to live victoriously, we must know what God's Word says about us. According to Psalm 8:5, we are crowned with glory and honor. Ephesians 2:6 says that we are seated with Christ in the heavenly realm. God sees us as we really are—clothed in righteousness with a crown of beauty on our head—and so does the enemy. Satan will do anything he can to keep us from seeing who we really are. He is constantly spurting out lies about what we are not and what we cannot do; whether we believe him is up to us. We are who God says we are, but we will never rise above the image we have of ourselves. While in the desert, the Israelites said, "And we were in our own sight as grasshoppers, and so we were in their sight" (Numbers 13:33 KJV). We have to recognize the enemy's lies and then change the way we think about ourselves in our minds and the way we believe about ourselves in our hearts. When we know who we are in Christ, we will exude a kind of beauty seen only in those who have truly been set free.

I have spent most of my time in ministry trying to help people see the true image of God. The good, faithful, true, loving, and forgiving God whom I have come to know is who I want everyone else to know. The God we have the ability to know and serve is beyond our wildest dreams. No wonder the enemy does everything he can to make us doubt God and his goodness. We have to trust God and resist the enemy. Part of building a strong foundation is learning to replace the enemy's lies with the truth of God's Word.

God remains true to his character regardless of how we see him or how we see ourselves. The story of Hosea and Gomer in the Bible is a perfect picture of God's unfailing love. God instructed the prophet Hosea to marry a prostitute named Gomer whose whole life was built on a broken foundation because of a warped image of God. Unfortunately, Gomer didn't see herself any differently when she was bought out of prostitution, and as a result, kept going back to her old way of life. She was more comfortable with the life she knew as a prostitute than with her new life as a prophet's wife. God instructed Hosea to buy her back each time she returned to prostitution because even though Gomer belonged to him, Hosea still had to buy her back. In much the same way, God sent his Son to buy us back, and like Gomer, we sometimes return to our old ways of life, and God has to come after us. His loving-kindness draws us to repentance. The good news is that he always takes us back, no matter how many times we forsake him and go our own way. God loves us unconditionally.

Another example of our Father's heart and what we mean to him is clearly depicted in the story of the prodigal son. The wayward son had squandered his inheritance, ending up poor and alone. He was tending pigs to earn some money when he realized that his father's hired servants were living a better life than he was, so he decided to return home, thinking he could at least work for his father as a hired servant. He no longer saw himself as a son and did not expect to be treated as one. The scripture tells us, however, that the father was eagerly looking for his son and saw him even while he was far off and ran to meet him and embraced him with open arms. The father immediately clothed the wayward son with one of his finest robes, put a ring on his finger, and then threw a bash to celebrate his return. All the son had to do was simply receive what his father offered him.

We have all gone astray and sometimes feel like the prodigal son. We feel muddied by our mistakes and waste our time tending pigs. We don't see ourselves as God's children anymore, and we expect very little.

Examine your life to see what pigs you are tending. Let go of the messes, whether you made them or someone else did. We are still children of the King and have a glorious inheritance. We have only to return home and receive the abundant life our heavenly Father is offering us.

Second Samuel 22:36 in the NIV says, "You give me your shield of victory; you stoop down to make me great." That scripture reminds me of the picture my sister took of my niece and her father years ago. My niece was running toward her father, who was kneeling on the ground with arms stretched wide. My sister snapped the photo the moment the child reached her father's open arms. You could see pure joy on both of their faces. Our heavenly Father stoops down to embrace us in the same way; we too are his beloved children.

Although we often lose sight of our true selves when we encounter difficult and painful circumstances in life, God never does. He knows the potential within us; after all, he put it there. From the beginning of time, he has had a plan for our restoration. Scripture says God created us for his glory. You and I were intricately formed and uniquely fashioned by God, for God. We were created to glorify our Creator! No matter who we are, we have a purpose in life. We are people of destiny. Nothing glorifies God more than us fulfilling our destinies and becoming all we were created to be. We in turn are happiest and most content as we fulfill the plans and purposes God has for our lives.

As we come to know God and his ways, we can learn to run to him as our refuge when we face pain and disappointment in life. Psalm 9:9 refers to the

Lord as a stronghold (strength, protector) in times of trouble. God wants to be our provider and protector. He alone is the correct stronghold. God wants us to be free from the strongholds that keep us captive so that we can rightly relate to him and his Word.

The more we know and understand God, the more freedom we will walk in. Deliverance from captivity is a process. It's not that God can't immediately and completely deliver us; he does. However, sometimes it takes us a while to appropriate that freedom. Truly, it does take time to learn how to function in freedom. God will not leave you alone to flounder. His development and training are a thorough process. Isaiah 28:10 shows us that God builds precept upon precept and line upon line. Another reason for God allowing us to take the route of process rather than sudden deliverance is that he uses our experiences of inner healing and deliverance to benefit others. In our times of growing in freedom, we develop faith in the areas we are overcoming. We have something to offer others because of what we have been through. We can encourage and help them to grow in faith as we have.

In the chapters ahead, I shall share the root causes of strongholds that the Lord has shown me, but I want to challenge you to look honestly at how you deal with pain to be free. I cannot do it for you, and neither can anyone else. You have to know the truth for yourselves and begin to apply it in your lives. My fervent prayer is that you will allow the Lord to break through your strongholds so that he can begin to repair your broken and cracked foundations.

Dear precious Lord, I give you permission to fix my foundation. Break down and remove the lies in my heart and replace them with truth. Amen

The Grace of God

give up. I am doing everything I know to do. I pray, read the Bible, and attend church twice a week. I sing in the choir and serve in the children's ministry, yet it never seems to be enough. I always fall short, no matter how hard I try. I do not know why I even bother.

Does this story sound familiar to you? If I have heard this statement once, I must have heard it hundreds, if not thousands, of times, particularly from those who have come to me for counseling through the years. It may come as a surprise, but many of the people who have said these words have been walking with the Lord for a long time. It's possible that you might feel the same way they do, and if you do, then it is imperative right here and now to remind you that ours is not a gospel of works but one of grace. Jesus has already accomplished all the works that we will ever need—on the cross.

That which is required of us is to just accept it by faith. We try to do things on our own and then grumble and complain when we do not get our way or if it is taking longer than expected. We become discouraged on the journey and lose sight of the destination. What actually happens is that we forget who we are and what is rightfully ours as children of the most high God.

The Performance Trap

Many Christians resort to performance because they do not understand God's grace. We have been indoctrinated our entire lives with a works mentality, where people are rewarded based on their performance. Across the board, our experiences and environment have conditioned us to perform. As a result, like little circus poodles, we tend to get stuck in works of the flesh, which ultimately have no reward.

> Know that a man is not justified by observing the law, but by faith in Jesus Christ.
>
> Galatians 2:16 (NIV)

The gospel is called the *good news* for a reason, and salvation is not based on our own efforts. "For by grace you have been saved, through faith" (Ephesians 2:8 NKJV). If we could have done something on our own merit to get to God, then Jesus would not have had to die the way he did. God made the way for us to be reconciled to him in spite of our sin. "For there is one God and one mediator between God and men, the man Christ Jesus" (1 Timothy 2:5 KJV). We can now have a personal relationship with God because of what he accomplished through Christ on the cross. God authored the liberating power of forgiveness so we could draw near to him, and because of the work Jesus accomplished on Calvary, we now have unreserved access to our Father. Like little children, you and I can come into his presence even when we mess up. It is when we know and believe the Lord that we can approach him in confidence and full assurance of faith, knowing that our sins have already been forgiven.

At first, it is hard for us to fathom how God can forgive us for all the awful things we have done, and it almost seems too good to be true, but it is. The Bible says that God is not holding our trespasses against us. According to Psalm 103:12, God has removed our sins from us as far as the east is from the west. He remembers them no more. Jesus paid for our sins in full when he suffered, died on the cross, and rose again. He paid for the sins we committed yesterday and today, as well as those we will commit in the future. Knowing that we are completely forgiven by God for every sin we have ever committed, or ever will commit, is the most important aspect of God's grace. We have been washed clean from all iniquities, trespasses, and sins. When God looks at us, he sees us through the precious blood of Jesus. We are blameless and pure in his sight. It is only by God's grace that we are forgiven, delivered, and set free.

God's grace is by far the greatest gift that we have received from the Lord. I am still amazed by it after all these years. God's grace is more than just forgiveness for our sins; it is God's unmerited favor and spiritual blessing; it is his willingness to be involved in our lives. God shows his love for us by the grace he pours out on us. God knows how much we need his grace, and he issues it for every necessity and desire. God gives us grace to wake up and get out of bed in the morning and to get through the day. God gives us grace to deal with screaming children, job demands, and imperfect spouses.

Grace works in our lives through faith. We have to believe and accept the grace God offers us because we cannot earn it. We must take hold of the grace of God because it is a free gift. We can embrace each new day knowing that God's grace will meet us right where we are. Having a grateful heart is the most important ingredient in helping us remain strong in faith and receptive to God's grace. So often we are like the temperamental Israelites who complained about not having any meat rather than thanking God for the manna that fell down fresh from heaven every day. They then proceeded to question God as to why he had delivered them out of Egypt to let them die in the desert. Like many counselors, I too have heard so many people question God when their lives are not going well.

Contrary to their twisted belief, however, God is

not the problem. God is good, and he truly is good all of the time. According to James 1:17, every good and perfect gift comes from God. In the garden, Adam and Eve fell for the lie that God was somehow holding out on them, and unfortunately, this same lie continues to work in some of God's people. We have been fighting it for centuries and are still so often deceived. At one end of the deceit spectrum are the small disappointments and things that we have believed God for that have not yet come to pass, and at the other end is the attitude that *I have done my part* (e.g., prayed the right prayers, read the right books, obeyed the Word), *but God has not done his part.* The truth is that God is not the problem. He does not tempt us, and though his timing might be different from ours, he is good. Isaiah 30:18 (AMP) says, "The Lord [earnestly] waits [expecting, looking, and longing] to be gracious to you."

According to Psalm 84:11 (NKJV), "No good thing will He withhold from those who walk uprightly."

I lived a lot of years believing that God was holding out on me and consequently dug a hole for myself by believing this lie. We find it easier to blame God for the things that are not going our way rather than to take responsibility for our own actions. People who feel like there is nothing else they can do are deceived into thinking that God has not done his part. That is nonsense. Jesus took all of our sin and shame when he went to the cross. He was wounded for our transgressions, and by his stripes we are healed. Through Christ's sacrifice on the cross, God has done everything that he is going to do. All that has been given to us in Christ is available to every person on this earth. We simply must take him up on it, and we must believe that what he says is true and has truly been accomplished.

Most Christians believe that they have to measure up in some way to be acceptable to the Lord. The truth is that we can never measure up. We do not deserve anything from God, even on our best days. God is holy, and we as human beings could never earn our way to God or earn anything from God. Nothing we could do in our own strength would make us acceptable to the Lord. We could never be holy on our own, yet the Lord has made us acceptable through Christ, and his Spirit makes us holy.

I am grieved when I see people believe the lies I used to believe. I used to live with the false sense of hopelessness that comes when you are in that catch-22 situation and cannot break through to the victory on the other side. So many people are waiting for God to do or show them something, and all the while, God is waiting for them to grasp the truth of what he has already done. Before he reveals a new revelation to you, he wants to know what you are going to do with the one you've got. Now, I am not denying that we face tough questions in life, such as *when will I find a better job,* or *what will it take to restore the relationship with my loved one,* or *how long will these symptoms persist in my body?* But as we wait to see the fruition of God's promises in our lives, we have to continue on the journey and keep believing that God is not holding out on us.

Galatians 3:3 (NKJV) asks, "Are you so foolish? Having begun in the Spirit are you now being made perfect by the flesh?" Our Christian walk began the moment we believed what Christ did for us and accepted the free gift of salvation, and we will finish our Christian walk the same way we started it—by believing what Christ did for us. This means that there is nothing we can do in the flesh to save or perfect ourselves. There is nothing we can do to measure up. We need God, and we need what his Son did for us.

You may be asking the same questions I asked for years. *What will it take to see the good news truly at work in my life, and why am I not living the abundant life Christ died to give me?* Although it is not complex, the answers to these questions have eluded far too many for far too long, and it is simply that we must humble ourselves. Humbling ourselves just means acknowledging that we cannot ever stand before a holy God on our own merit. For those who are self-sufficient and pride themselves on their accomplishments and their spirit of independence, this may be extremely difficult to do. Moreover, it may even sound rather hopeless to the world, but as believers, we know our hope is in Christ. We can come boldly to the throne of grace because of what Christ has done for us.

Grace Brings Breakthrough

The breakthrough that we are all looking for comes when we humbly accept the payment Christ made for our sins. The Word tells us that God opposes the proud but gives grace to the humble. The block we feel when we are trying to do it ourselves is God's opposition. Proverbs 13:10 (KJV) says, "Only by pride cometh contention." We oppose God when we put our confidence in ourselves. Our confidence has to be in God and what he has accomplished for us.

Humility means *I need God.* I need him to breathe, to minister, to be a wife and a mother, and I need him to help me through each and every day. I have often heard the world remark that Christians are weak and that only weak people need a savior. Well, I would have to agree with them, for Christ came to save the weak and needy. I think we are all surprised when we discover how weak and in need of God we really are. Even the most autonomous personalities will eventually find themselves in situations where their money, fame, or status cannot get them out easily. Yes, we are all hopelessly and helplessly in need of a savior. We need his grace, not just once, but over and over again. It's a continual and unending supply. You see, it is the people who know they need God and that they need a savior who are the ones who will walk in the fullness of God's abundant grace. True humility is recognizing that our worth comes from God alone. We accomplish nothing without his power, guidance, and provision. Even our gifts and talents come from him.

> Lord, you establish peace for us; all that we have accomplished you have done for us.
>
> Isaiah 26:12 (NIV)

Although we often get frustrated with one another, God never gives up on us. He promises that his mercy is new every day and simply requires that we take him up on it. While we are getting to know God and learning to trust him, we can rest assured that his great mercy will meet us each morning.

> Surely or only goodness, mercy and unfailing love shall follow me all the days of my life, and through the length of my days the house of the Lord (and His presence) shall be my dwelling place.
>
> Psalm 23:6 (AMP)

Just before Jesus gave up his life on the cross, he cried out, "It is finished" (John 19:30 KJV). So if Christ Jesus, the King of kings and the Lord of lords, pronounced that it is finished, then we must allow it to be finished. We must honor what he has done by accepting his shed blood as enough for our sins and the sins of those who have hurt us. If we do not accept God's forgiveness, we can become captive to the stronghold of condemnation. Condemnation is the judgment of our sin upon us. Just imagine a judge slamming a gavel down in a courtroom, yelling, "Guilty as charged!" Once condemned, the defendant is helpless and hopeless to change the verdict.

> Therefore there is now no condemnation for those who are in Christ Jesus.
>
> Romans 8:1 (NAS)

Condemnation is not from the Lord, not ever. It's not in his nature. We must recognize the difference between condemnation from the enemy and conviction from the Holy Spirit. Condemnation is vague, points at us rather than the sin, and offers no hope of escape, while the Lord's conviction is clear, points directly to the sin, and always offers hope and a way out.

If we do not respond quickly to the Lord's conviction, the enemy will bring condemnation, which may come either from within or from someone else. Condemnation comes when we do not take Christ up on what he did. We must allow ourselves to be forgiven because if we do not know that we are forgiven in Christ, we will run from the Lord when convicted. If we rely on God's grace to forgive us, we will deal with the Holy Spirit's conviction by turning to him, and this will allow us to move on quickly and in freedom.

Experience has shown that those who condemn themselves are more likely to condemn others, which perpetuates the cycle of pain and bondage. We get to choose whether we will accept God's forgiveness and move on or wallow in guilt and condemnation. Trust is the bottom line. Are we going to take God at his word? We must act on what we know to be the truth—God's Word—and not our feelings because we are forgiven regardless of how we feel. It requires humility to believe God's Word over our own feelings of doubt and unbelief. When we disregard the conviction of the Holy Spirit, we are making a choice not to own our sins. Ignoring conviction is dangerous because our hearts harden over time and become less sensitive to the prompting of the Holy Spirit.

I lived under condemnation for most of my life. I was truly sorry for my sins but thought I had to somehow pay for them. I learned as a child that if I felt bad enough about my mistakes, I might not be punished, and I thought this was true in my relationship with God. I thought I had to feel bad about myself to avoid being punished, so for a long time, I felt unworthy and inferior, and I had an inherent disdain toward myself.

Before I understood the exchange that Christ made for me at the cross, I tried to earn my way back to God every time I sinned. I used to make lists of everything I had done wrong and repent over and over, yet I never felt better. I could not rid myself of the guilt. I told my mentor and friend about my battle with condemnation, and she asked me not to repent often for days but to rest in what I knew God had done for me. You cannot imagine how hard that was for me. When I repeatedly asked for the Lord's forgiveness, I felt like I was doing something. Repentance was a place of safety for me, yet another twisted lure into the performance trap, and this particular trap was easy to fall into because repentance, for me at least, was a religious act.

After a week of not begging for the Lord's forgiveness, I realized I had survived and that God still loved me. Instead of repenting, I had taken communion. I began to understand that Christ had taken my sin to the cross. I remember the day that I finally got it. I read these words in Galatians 3:3 (KJV): "Are (you) ye so foolish? Having begun in the Spirit, are ye now made perfect by the flesh?" That question opened my eyes to the fact that I had been saved simply by God's grace. Although I desire to grow in holiness, the rest of my walk with the Lord is still about receiving his grace. If we are not good enough to save ourselves, we will certainly not be good enough to earn anything else from the Lord. If we could have saved ourselves without him, he would not have had to die for our sins.

> If we confess our sins, he is faithful and just to forgive us our sins, and to cleanse us from all unrighteousness.
>
> 1 John 1:9 (KJV)

Confessing our sins is more than mentally assenting to what we have done; it is agreeing with God that what we have done is wrong and desiring to change. Real change takes place in our lives when we admit our sin and turn from it (repentance), and in his great mercy, God forgives and cleanses us repeatedly.

God's grace is not a license to sin or live a sloppy life. He still requires us to be responsible and does not want our sacrifices or works of the flesh, but he wants our obedience. Performance and obedience are two different things. The benefits of being in a right relationship with God are not predicated by our obedience. We obey the Lord because we love him, not because we can earn anything from him. God does not stop loving us when we disobey him, but it does, however, break his heart because he knows the natural consequences that follow our disobedience.

As believers in Christ, we do not have to perform for the love God has for us. His love is a gift we do not have to earn. We must not waste time beating ourselves up over our sins. Christ has taken our sin to the cross. It does not matter how we feel. What matters is what God's Word says. If God says we are forgiven, then we are forgiven; take him at his word. We need to express our gratitude by believing what Christ has done for us and by taking him up on his promises. God is not mad at us. If we are afraid that we are in trouble, we are not walking in faith. We must become secure in the fact that God loves us and will not give up on us, no matter how many mistakes we make. The best way to become secure in who we are in Christ is to spend time in God's Word and in prayer.

When I make a mistake now, I go to the Lord in prayer and say, "Lord, this is what I did. I am so sorry. I repent and ask for your forgiveness. I thank you from the bottom of my heart that according to 1 John 1:9, you are faithful and just to forgive me. Your blood is enough." And I am done. No more lists, no more begging, no more guilt and condemnation.

It took me years to begin to understand God's grace. When we walk according to the law rather than grace, we set up standards for ourselves that we cannot meet, and we establish the same rules and standards for other people. I was so afraid of this mean, angry God whom I thought was punishing my family and me, and I saw God as a harsh taskmaster whom I could never please, no matter what I did. I wrongly accused him of orchestrating the hurts and disappointments I faced in life, and because of these false beliefs, I lived under fear and condemnation. I could not draw close to God in prayer.

The truth is that God is not mean, nor mad at you, but is kind and compassionate. His love and mercy endure forever. God loves us and cares about every aspect of our lives. When I allowed those truths to sink into my heart, my life changed. I hope your life will be changed too after hearing these truths.

We need to remind ourselves of God's grace on a regular basis. We must never let go of what Christ did for us at the cross. We need to read and study the many wonderful books that have been written on God's grace so that we never forget just how amazing it is.

Understanding God's grace will help prepare us for the chapters ahead. God's grace is required to overcome strongholds like unforgiveness, rejection, fear, doubt, and unbelief. When we do not receive God's grace, it is hard for us to move beyond our past and to trust that he has good things in store for our future. God wants us to be healed of our past hurts and wounds, because if we are just pretending to be over them, they will come back to bite us somewhere down the road. Are you ready to move past your past? If you are, you will be happiest and most content as you live the life God intended for you to live. God is pleased as we believe and accept what he has done for us. What we do with what he has given us is our gift to him. God is glorified when we walk in ever-increasing levels of freedom.

Today, thank God for his unfailing love, forgiveness, and grace. When you do not perform perfectly, march right back into his presence; he loves us just as we are and will always take us back. He is transforming us into his image and promises to complete the work he has begun.

> If we are faithless, He remains true (faithful to His Word and His righteous character), for He cannot deny Himself.
>
> 2 Timothy 2:13 (AMP)

In other words, he is going to be true to his Word and its effects working in us. He is going to love us regardless of what we have or have not done. For lack of a better word, he just can't help himself. We are the object of his undying love and affection, and when we finally believe and receive that as truth and reality in our lives, we are going to start to climb higher!

Dear precious Lord, help me to know and accept your amazing grace.

The Key to All Freedom

Somewhere along the line, we have to grow up and address the unresolved hurts of the past. While it may seem easier to take the stance that it's just water under the bridge and let bygones be bygones so that we can move on from here, the truth is that one really does not simply move on. Nor can a person just quickly brush these issues beneath the rug because they will inevitably resurface again, and the next time the hurt will be harder to manage. Rather than ignore our sleeping giants, we must allow the Lord to arouse these fiends from their slumber and oust them out of our lives, and the vehicle that God uses to break us free from the chains of our bondage is forgiveness.

Now, I know that this might seem overly simplistic to say that forgiveness is the key instrument God uses to bring his children to freedom, but it is. I, for one, can personally testify that forgiveness has been the key to all freedom in my life. It was only when I learned to forgive those who hurt me and let go of the pain that I was finally able to heal properly and move on. Forgiveness made a way for me to embrace the life God had in store for me, and I hope you will allow forgiveness to clear the path for you too.

Misconceptions of Forgiveness

One of the reasons people struggle with forgiving others is the mistaken belief that if they do, they are somehow admitting that they were wrong and that the perpetrator was right. This couldn't be further from the truth. Forgiveness has more to do with us than the other person. You see, unforgiveness becomes a wall or barrier that keeps us from entering into God's presence, and as such, forgiveness is the only thing that can tear down the wall and restore open communication with our heavenly Father.

Mark 11:25–26 says that when we come to the Lord in prayer, we must first forgive others. Jesus went on to say in Matthew 6:15 that if we don't forgive others' sins, our sins will not be forgiven. Seriously then, how can we expect God to release us from the effects of past pains and hurts when we insist on holding onto them? One of the most sobering scriptures I have ever encountered regarding the consequence of not forgiving is this: Jesus said in John 20:23 (NKJV),

" … if you forgive the sins of any, they are forgiven them; if you retain the sins of any, they are retained." There is a great deal of conflicting commentary written from multiple perspectives on what exactly this verse is conveying, but I think that the verse simply means this: The sins that we release through forgiveness in turn release us, but the sins we retain and hold onto become our prison cells.

Unforgiveness is always accompanied by bondage. Its sole intent is to enslave us, and if we entertain and pander to it long enough, we will eventually look up one day only to discover that we are encased in bars. Although Christ continues to reach out to us, the bars have a way of deceiving and eventually convincing us that we are unapproachable, unworthy, and unloved. Soon we may find ourselves unable to draw near to God and to ask for forgiveness in our own hearts; therefore, those sins are not forgiven. This is not because God has walled us out but because we have walled ourselves in. Thus, by our own stubborn admission, we insulate ourselves from receiving the love of God and his forgiveness.

We are fooling ourselves if we think that holding on to a grudge or executing swift vengeance and judgment is somehow sweet recompense. On the contrary, we are just inviting ourselves into bondage. There are too many health benefits that we are forfeiting by holding onto our right to offense and unforgiveness. Today, doctors can medically link cancer to some issues regarding unforgiveness. Unforgiveness is not a luxury, and we certainly cannot afford it. It is far too costly physically and emotionally to allow its presence in our lives. God commands us to forgive others for a reason. He knows the destructive consequences that come when we break his spiritual laws, and whether we realize it or not, the law of sowing and reaping is always in motion. If we sow unforgiveness, we will reap the effects of unforgiveness, which include bondage. You see, God is aware of the danger we put ourselves in when we do not forgive. He knows what causes us to stumble and fall; therefore, his laws help us to be alert and on guard.

Think about when we were children. It is likely that our mothers told us not to run into the street. They were not telling us this to be mean or to keep us from having fun; they did not want us to get hurt. Their instructions were intended to keep us safe. God is the same way. He is our heavenly Father and has our best interests at heart. Whenever God commands us to do something, it is always for our good and our protection.

I believe we struggle to forgive others because we do not understand what it truly means to forgive. Real, honest forgiveness is a choice, not a feeling, and is an act of our will—a decision of the heart to completely let go of wounds and overlook or pardon offenses. To forgive is to treat the offender as not guilty. Does this mean that what the offender did to us was not wrong? No. It is wrong for people knowingly, or unknowingly, to hurt one another. True forgiveness acknowledges that what the offender did was wrong but hands the responsibility of making it right to God.

We might think forgiveness lets the offender off the hook, when in actuality forgiveness lets us off the hook. When we do not forgive someone, we remain emotionally tied to that person. He may not even know he has hurt us, and yet we carry him around wherever we go. We often think we are making the offender pay by not forgiving him. How silly is that? It is like drinking poison and hoping the other person will die! When we forgive him, we free ourselves from a burden God never intended us to carry. Forgiveness frees us.

Our job is to forgive. God's job is to deal with the other person. We are not to seek vengeance because God is our vindicator. He is a big God who is more than able to bring justice to every unfair situation. God knows the hurts we have suffered, and he promises to compensate us. No matter what we have lost, God promises to restore double to us.

> Instead of your [former] shame you shall have a twofold recompense.
>
> Isaiah 61:7 (AMP)

Forgiveness actually opens the door for the Lord to work in the heart of the other person, and at the same time restore to us what has been lost in our hearts. God loves the people who have wronged us, and offers them the same grace he offers us. He allows them time to repent and return to him.

We tend to hold on to hurts because it gives us a sense of control. Unfortunately, the exact opposite is true. Holding onto the pain makes it possible for the

offender to control us. Think about it this way: If we
constantly dwell on how a parent hurt us as a child,
he or she is controlling our minds; if we stay angry
and upset with a friend, he or she is controlling our
emotions; if we go out of our way to avoid an ex-
husband, he is controlling our actions. We can even
allow people who are no longer alive to control us.

The Bible says we are to be controlled by the
Holy Spirit and not man. In order to surrender to
the Holy Spirit, we must first take back any control
in our lives that we have given to others. When we
forgive others, the false sense of control we felt by
holding onto the hurt is restored as proper responsibility for ourselves. Forgiveness frees us to take control of our lives.

Matthew 18:21–35 (NIV) offers us some of the
greatest insight into forgiveness:

> Then Peter came to Jesus and asked, "Lord, how
> many times shall I forgive my brother when
> he sins against me? Up to seven times?" Jesus
> answered, "I tell you, not seven times, but seventy
> times seven. Therefore, the kingdom of heaven is
> like a king who wanted to settle accounts with
> his servants. As he began the settlement, a man
> who owed him ten thousand talents was brought
> to him. Since he was not able to pay, the master
> ordered that he and his wife and his children and
> all that he had be sold to repay the debt. The ser-
> vant fell on his knees before him. "Be patient with
> me," he begged, "and I will pay back everything."
> The servant's master took pity on him, canceled
> the debt and let him go. But when that servant

went out, he found one of his fellow servants who owed him a hundred denarii. He grabbed him and began to choke him. "Pay back what you owe me!" he demanded. His fellow servant fell to his knees and begged him, "Be patient with me, and I will pay you back." But he refused. Instead, he went off and had the man thrown into prison until he could pay the debt. When the other servants saw what had happened, they were greatly distressed and went and told their master everything that had happened. Then the master called the servant in. "You wicked servant," he said, "I canceled all that debt of yours because you begged me to. Shouldn't you have had mercy on your fellow servant just as I had on you?" In his anger his master turned him over to the jailers to be tortured, until he should pay back all he owed. This is how my heavenly Father will treat each of you unless you forgive your brother from your heart.

The passage opens with an example of how we as humans struggle to be merciful to others. Peter asked the Lord how many times he should forgive his brother. It sounds like Peter was looking for a formula. Was seven times enough? He wanted to be able to say, "Lord, after seven times, can I just quit and be done with the other person?" The Lord responded, "Forgive not just seven times but seventy times seven."

The number seven is significant because it stands for completion. So when he went on to say, "Seventy times seven" imagine the simple yet profound message he was conveying. Christ was saying in essence,

"Let forgiveness be a way of life for you. Make love your highest aim. Let this be a lifestyle issue for you. Be ready to forgive." Furthermore, Jesus was saying, "There is no limit. Keep on forgiving."

Like Peter, we often want to limit our forgiveness and hold the offenders responsible for what they have done. However, that is not God's way. Christ died for us while we were yet sinners (Romans 5:8). His mercy is endless. God forgives us no matter how many times we mess up, and we should forgive others in the same way. "Be gentle and forbearing with one another and, if one has a difference (a grievance or complaint) against another, readily pardoning each other; even as the Lord has [freely] forgiven you, so must you also [forgive]" (Colossians 3:13 AMP). We must choose to forgive others on a daily basis if we want to find freedom and walk in it.

The story of the rich king and the servant in Matthew 18 is meant to show us the enormous difference between what we are expected to forgive and what the Lord has forgiven. Just like the master who canceled the servant's debt, Jesus paid a debt that we could not pay. He became the propitiation (full payment) for our sins. The servant had been released from an enormous debt, yet the debt he refused to pardon—that of his fellow servant—was insignificant in comparison. Likewise, the forgiveness required of us is small compared to the forgiveness God has shown us. We are often deluded into thinking that what we did was not as bad as what the other person did to us. Even if that is the case, we need to remind ourselves that we are forgiven. God not only forgives our sinful actions; he also forgives every one of our sinful, selfish, and unkind thoughts and words.

I used to think it was odd that the first servant put his fellow servant in jail until he could pay back what he owed because how is someone in prison supposed to earn the wages needed to pay back the debt? Then I realized that we often do the same thing. We put those who have hurt us into our own private prisons and think that shutting them behind bars will somehow force them to make things right. Yet the people who have hurt us cannot pay the debt either. It does not do any good to require those who have hurt us to make things right. No one can undo what has already been done. Apologies may help, but they cannot erase what has transpired.

Our forgiveness cannot be dependent on the other person's apology or effort to make things right. Even if he or she did apologize or try to remedy the wrong, something in our flesh would still require more; it wouldn't be enough. Over the years, I have seen countless people demand an apology before they would forgive. Some of these people are still waiting, and others will wait their entire lives. Again, this is not God's way. We are no longer living under the old covenant, which demanded an eye for an eye and a tooth for a tooth. We are living under the new covenant of God's grace. We have received God's unmerited favor and are called to extend that same favor to those who have hurt us. Who are we not to forgive others when God, who is holy, has forgiven us?

Called to Forgive

We are called and empowered to forgive others as we have been forgiven, and we do not necessarily have to forgive in person (face to face) because forgiveness is between God and us. When God forgives us, our slates are wiped clean. When we forgive others, we should clean their slates too. The Bible says love holds no record of wrong, and love is the greatest commandment in the kingdom of God. To experience release from bondage, we must forgive others quickly and completely. In Luke 11:4 (NIV), the Lord teaches us to pray: "Forgive us our sins, for we also forgive everyone who sins against us." We would be more likely to truly forgive others if we really understood what we were asking for when we pray the Lord's Prayer. Do we really want to be forgiven as we have forgiven others?

I also believe that if we could really see our sin for what it is, we would be more inclined to quickly forgive those who have sinned against us. Sin is sin. My sin is not worse than your sin; neither is yours worse than mine. "There is no one righteous, not even one" (Romans 3:10 NIV). I like to think of this as common corruption. After years of listening to horrible stories of people hurting one another, I realized that we are all capable of doing the same awful things. We would like to think that somehow we are better than those who have hurt us, but the truth is that we are not. Human nature is human nature, and no one is perfect. We may have made different choices, but we are all capable of making the same mistakes.

You never know what people have gone through that made them the way they are. They may have endured immense pain. While most people do not intend to hurt others, they often do so because they are hurting. I am not saying that the pain someone suffers excuses the pain they cause others but am simply saying that people usually have reasons for acting the way they do. When we understand this, it makes it easier to forgive. The person who hurt or let us down was probably hurt or let down by someone else. That person can only give what has ever been received and cannot give unconditional love if he or she has not personally received God's unconditional love.

The Cost of Not Forgiving

The last lesson from Matthew 18 has to do with God's spiritual law of sowing and reaping. Jesus said in Matthew 5:7 (KJV), "Blessed are the merciful, for they shall obtain mercy." The servant who would not forgive his fellow servant's debt was ultimately turned over to the jailers to be tortured. The torture we face as a result of unforgiveness is spiritual and mental, and such torment can eventually affect us physically. I have personally experienced the torment caused by unforgiveness and do not recommend it. If there is ever hell on earth, that is it. Nobody wants to live there, yet so many of us do. If you have ever experienced this torture, you know exactly what I am talking about.

Webster's Dictionary defines torture as *anguish of body or mind; agony; to twist, cause extreme pain, or torment.* Torment occurs because the enemy twists the truth. He bombards you with agonizing lies that cause confusion. Torment may be difficult to recognize because it looks different to each person. When I was tormented, I could not stop thinking about what happened to me. I tried to put those agonizing thoughts out of my mind, but they came right back. Once the torment begins, no one but you can stop it. Forgiveness is the only way out. If you recognize the symptoms of torment after reading this, ask the Lord to show you if there is someone you need to forgive. It only takes a minute yet can end hours of agony.

Unfortunately, the lesson on torment is one I had to learn the hard way. Years ago, I struggled to forgive someone who had hurt me. I prayed. I cried. I did everything I knew to do but could not get over the hurt. It felt like the pain was all over me, and nothing I did made it go away. I was miserable. The event played over and over in my mind. I analyzed and thought about it constantly. Although what happened was truly painful, I was not dealing with it correctly. I wanted the person who hurt me to make it right, although I am not sure what I expected that person to do. The truth is that I was hurting and wanted that person to hurt too. I wallowed in my hurt long enough to be tormented.

One day while I was going through this agonizing torment, a friend who truly loved and wanted God's best for me showed up at my door. She had been thinking and praying about me and knew she had to tell me the truth. We sat down together in my bedroom, and she said, "You have to forgive or you will continue to face this torment." I am sure it took a lot of courage for her to say those words to me, and they were not easy words to hear. It seemed like they slapped me in the face as soon as they left her mouth. I am grateful she loved me enough to tell me the truth; otherwise, I would have remained in torment. When I realized I was the only one who could put an end to the anguish, I decided to forgive immediately. The moment I forgave, the tormenting thoughts stopped.

That was the day I finally understood that forgiveness was both an act of my will and an act of my faith. We do not have to wait until we feel like forgiving; we make a decision to forgive and let offenses go regardless of our feelings. Often, we want to be led by our feelings, then the facts, and lastly by faith, but that is not God's way. We must know the truth, act on it, have faith in the truth we have acted on, and eventually, the feelings will follow. When we accept the truth that forgiveness brings freedom and make a decision by faith to forgive, God works to change our feelings, renew our minds, and restore our souls. God's ways are not our ways, but his ways are always best.

Often, we feel entitled to hold on to our hurts, but unforgiveness is not a right; it is a stronghold that keeps us in terrible bondage. Looking back, I can see clearly how unforgiveness was hurting me much more than it was hurting the other person. I was tormented, and all my relationships were suffering. I could not fully enjoy my husband, my children, or my friendships until I made the decision to forgive. When we realize that forgiveness sets us free from the hurts of our past, we are more apt to forgive quickly. I was holding the key to my freedom.

Equipped to Forgive

Real forgiveness is carried out with serious thought. It is neither mindless nor flippant, and it does not pretend things never happened. We must acknowledge the wrong to truly forgive it. Once we take an honest look at what happened and make a decision to let go of the wrong, we have to give the person and the pain to the Lord in prayer. We then move on. Moving on can mean different things in different situations. When a need for forgiveness arises in a relationship, it is always good to reflect upon what might need to change. We may realize that we are giving too much of our heart away in a friendship and start setting firmer boundaries. At other times, we may need to completely break ties because forgiveness does not always mean staying in the relationship and reconciling with the person who hurt us. We have to look honestly at the situation and seek God's wisdom. Returning to an abusive relationship, for example, would not be wise. It was never God's will for us to be abused or abnormally used. We have to forgive the abuser but do not have to continue subjecting ourselves to the abuse.

It is often difficult to forgive because we hold on to our hurt feelings and pain. Just as an accident can lead to physical injuries, incidents in life can leave us with emotional injuries. We have to stop rehearsing the negative things that have happened to us, both in our thoughts and especially in our words. We are holding on to and reinforcing the pain when we constantly think and talk about what happened to us.

There have been many times I have had to make the choice to forgive, but when I saw the person who hurt me, it seemed as if all the hurt and anger came rushing back. The Lord showed me in Isaiah 53:4 that Jesus bore our pain and carried our sorrows to the cross. Just like our sin, Jesus has already taken our pain—past, present, and future—to the cross. We must deal with our pain the same way we deal with sin. We must own it, repent, give it to the Lord, and allow the blood of Jesus to wash us clean. I have found that once I really lay the pain at the cross, then forgiveness is lasting. It's only when I hold onto the pain that it still has its hooks in me.

God is saying the same thing to you he said to me. *Do you want the pain as a trophy, or can I have it?* Give your pain to the Lord. He took it to the cross. Why are you still holding onto it? Understanding that the Lord took my pain to the cross changed my perception of forgiveness. Now, when I have to forgive someone, I always bring the pain to the Lord in prayer. Doing so allows me to truly forgive and let go of the hurt. Real forgiveness acknowledges that the pain someone caused us has been taken to the cross on our behalf. Pain loses its power over us when we give it to the Lord.

If we think we have forgiven yet are still being tormented, we might be dealing with offense, resentment, or bitterness, which are close relatives of unforgiveness, just harder to recognize. They are the results of not dealing properly with the pain attached to hurt. An offense is usually our initial response to an insult or wrongdoing. Although we have no control over others hurting us, we can control whether we become offended. Offense has a lot to do with our pride and ego. We get offended when others do not listen to what we have to say or step on our toes. We become offended when we accept in our heart the wrongs done, but taking something into our hearts that does not belong there is sin. We are not, under any circumstance, to take offense. It is one of the most destructive tools in Satan's arsenal, and we as believers have no right to succumb to it. It not only destroys us but those around us as well. Allowing offense in our hearts is like allowing rattlesnakes into our homes; that is how dangerous it is. Jesus was very specific when referring to offense. He addressed John the Baptist and said in Matthew 11:6 (NASB), "And blessed is he who does not take offense at Me." In other words, don't always expect things to go the way you want; rest in God's love and his plan for your life.

Resentment is a lingering feeling of ill will or indignation. Often, we become resentful when things do not go our way. We can resent a co-worker for getting a promotion or the telephone repairman for showing up late. No offense is too small to attend to. Proverbs 19:11 says it is our glory to overlook a transgression or an offense. If we do not deal with a repeated offense properly, we can become resentful. Unfortunately, too many of us are pros when it comes to resentment because we choose to hang onto offenses. Resentment is an underlying feeling of being wronged, insulted, or injured, which sneaks up on us because it seems like the normal way to deal with people who continually let us down. We have to give up resentment and consider the offense as recalled and annulled to truly forgive someone. We have to let go of offenses and resentment the same way we let go of hurts and wounds. Forgive the person who offends us, lay the offenses and resentment on the altar, and repent for becoming offended or resentful. If we hold on to offenses, they grow out of proportion and wound us more than they should and keep us in a place of unforgiveness.

When harbored or held in our heart, unforgiveness turns into bitterness, which is by far the ugliest member of the unforgiveness family. Bitterness is defined as *intensely unpleasant and expressive of severe pain, grief, or regret.* Bitterness is akin to hatred; its effects are ugly and far-reaching, and it essentially says, "Who are you to hurt me?" Bitterness changes both the way we see ourselves and the way we treat others. It poisons our thoughts, words, and actions. In an attempt to protect ourselves, our actions reflect the cry of our heart, "You won't hurt me again!"

Bitterness causes us to act especially differently toward the person who contributed to our pain and distress. We might become sarcastic, curt, or mean;

we can become sour, which in turn affects the way we look. Whatever is taking place in our hearts is reflected on our faces. Sometimes we feel we cannot help but be bitter; but we have to personally choose not to be.

> Strive to live in peace with everybody and pursue that consecration and holiness without which no one will (ever) see the Lord. Exercise foresight and be on the watch to look (after one another), to see that no one falls back from and fails to secure God's grace (His unmerited favor and spiritual blessing), in order that no root of resentment (rancor, bitterness, or hatred) shoots forth and causes trouble and bitter torment, and the many become contaminated and defiled by it.
> Hebrews 12:14–15 (AMP)

Bitterness changes the way we approach God. We may feel distant from God, but he has not pulled away from us; we have pulled away from him. We will not draw near to him with bitterness in our hearts because deep down we know it is wrong. So make a decision now to hand it to God and get rid of it. God commands us to live in peace because he desires so much for us to come close to him.

We have all known someone who was bitter. Once you understand bitterness, it is easy to spot. Bitterness propels the person to talk about his pain all of the time. He will tell anyone who will listen how badly he was hurt and how awful the other person is. The negative seeds come spewing out when least expected. Bitter people want us to know and believe that the person who hurt them is bad, and our agreement continues to feed their bitterness.

I will be the first to admit that we are all susceptible to bitterness and its destructive consequences. Bitterness certainly changed me. A long time ago, I found a mentor who took me under his wing. I completely trusted this person. He was training me in ministry, and I had put my heart in his hands. I bet you can imagine what happened. Yes, he let me down. He accused me of something I could not even comprehend at the time. I felt like the rug had been pulled out from under me. I was hurt badly because I thought this person was for me. At the time, I did not know to go to the Lord and ask him if the accusation was true. The man's opinion wounded me deeply, and it took years for me to completely get over what had happened. The deeper the wound, the harder it is to let go and receive healing. I tried to forgive this man but just could not. I did not realize that I was holding onto the pain and had no idea that I had a choice to let it go.

Because I did not deal with the hurt properly, it manifested into full-fledged bitterness. I talked about it and thought about it all the time. It began to consume me. I was young in my walk with the Lord and did not know how to handle that kind of hurt. I did not know the biblical principle found in Matthew 18:15 that instructs us to resolve conflict by directly confronting the person involved. I was afraid that if I approached the man, he would hurt me again, so

I stewed in my bitterness for ages. It was not long before I found someone else who was also bitter at the same man, and we quickly became friends; after all, like minds are drawn to one another. This girl and I had bitter parties all the time. Every time we got together, we talked about this man and our wounds, and the more we focused on the incident, the larger it became in our minds. The saddest part about this story is that the man who wrongly accused me had no idea how badly he had hurt me.

A year after I had talked about the hurt with anyone who would listen, another pastor at the church told me the truth—I was bitter. I was surprised because I could not see what had taken root in my heart. I thought I was just trying to get well, but I had been deceived. Fortunately, I had learned by then to bring the accusation before the Lord and ask him what he thought about it. Within a couple of days, the Lord revealed to me just how bitter I had become. The passage in Hebrews 12:15 that states, "And thereby many be defiled" stared me in the face. I had defiled every person I had talked to about the incident and did not realize that I had planted a seed of doubt about this man in the heart of every person with whom I had spoken. I saw plenty of people who changed their opinion of that man based on the seeds I planted. Even those people who did not agree with me had received negative seeds that eventually produced rotten fruit in their lives.

I was heartbroken over what I had done. I went to the sanctuary and cried for three hours straight. I felt like I had opened a feather pillow and dumped it out of an airplane in midair. There was no way I could pick up all the feathers. I could not undo the damage I had caused, but I could trust God to heal what I had broken. I forgave the man for hurting me and apologized for what I had done. He forgave me for how I reacted to his original accusation. Realizing that hurting people hurt people made it easier for us to forgive each other. We reconciled, and our relationship was restored to the glory of God.

It is so important to examine what is in your heart on a daily basis. If you do not remove the root of bitterness, it will continue growing and producing bitter fruit. Uprooting bitterness from our hearts requires that we take a genuine look at ourselves and repent for having allowed bitterness in. We must choose to forgive the person, let go of the offense, and give the pain to the Lord. God's grace is the only antidote for bitterness, and we receive it by faith when we humble ourselves.

The damage that unforgiveness wreaks on families is enormous. If you have a stronghold of unforgiveness in your life, it will impact every relationship you have. Before I allowed God to heal me, I was not the mom or the wife I should have been. My wounds had changed me. Everyone around me paid in some way because I was hurt, angry, and afraid. Besides that, I did not like myself, which made it difficult for me to be happy. I wish I could have those years over, but I cannot. I wish I had known years ago what I know now about forgiveness and healing. I could have spared my loved ones and myself a lot of grief. I hurt many people because I was hurting.

In addition to forgiving the people who hurt me, I had to ask the people I hurt to forgive me for my mistakes. I will never forget my oldest son's response. He was nine years old at the time. He put his hand on my shoulder and said, "We are all human." That is how we should treat one another. If the people I hurt had not forgiven me, our family would have remained divided, and everyone would have suffered. Thankfully, God healed me and restored my relationships. Without forgiveness in place, we will not experience the healing, restoration, and wholeness we desire or that God desires for our relationships.

You might be wondering about forgiving yourself. When we confess our sins to God, we must let go of them and allow the Lord to wash us clean by faith. We cannot undo the mistakes we made in the past, but we can repent and allow his forgiveness to be enough. Who are we to hold ourselves guilty for something the Lord has forgiven? When we truly accept the Lord's forgiveness and allow him to cleanse us, we will not need to forgive ourselves. Understanding that God loves us unconditionally in spite of our sins frees us to be who we were created to be. Freedom comes to those who allow the Lord to accomplish the work he was sent to do in their lives. Jesus paid the penalty for our sins when he was crucified on the cross and rose from the grave; he bought our salvation. Accept the fullness of this salvation. When I see Jesus face to face, I want him to say, "You took me up on everything I died to give you." What about you?

When we struggle to forgive someone who has hurt or let us down, we need to go back to the cross and remember how God has forgiven us completely. Accept his grace and extend that same grace to others. Writing a letter to the person who hurt us can also help start the process of forgiveness within; just do not send the letter because it would do more harm than good. We do not want to cause others pain in our attempts to forgive. The goal is to heal our heart, not hurt someone else, and the unsent letter serves as an avenue for us to pour out our emotions about the wound or offense.

It is similar to what David did when he expressed his deepest emotions and pain in the psalms. I recommend writing down everything you have ever wanted to say to that person, including all of the emotions you felt or still feel, and write how the event changed you. After you have written your letter, choose to forgive that person. Remember to give the pain to the Lord. You will be amazed at what forgiveness will do for you. You never know what is on the other side of simple obedience, but you can be assured that when you adhere to biblical principles like forgiveness, you will always be blessed. The body of Christ would look so different if Christians really forgave each other. I hope you will let the change start with you.

God wants us to be free so we can fulfill our destiny, and the key to our freedom is forgiveness.

I encourage you to pray about the truths you have learned in this chapter. In the paragraph below, you will find a simple prayer to help you to get started. Take time to deal with anything the Lord brings to the surface. You do not have to dig things up from your past; the Lord will show you what you need to deal with when the time is right. Moreover, you will have the grace to deal with any sin or stronghold the Lord reveals to you. However, I want to caution you in this: You will not have the same grace to deal with issues you dig up yourself that the Lord is not dealing with at the moment. Beloved, know that I am praying with you and for you.

Lord, I thank you for forgiving me and for bestowing your mercy and grace on me. Help me to recognize whom I need to forgive. Show me specific hurts I need to forgive and how these hurts have changed me. Help me open my heart to your healing. Show me any pain I am holding onto and help me to release this pain. Soften my heart to your voice of conviction. Empower me by your Holy Spirit to forgive as you do. Help me to rest in what you have done for me, knowing, "It is finished." Amen.

With forgiveness in place, you are now ready to move forward. In the chapters ahead, we will look at other strongholds that may be keeping you in bondage and how you can overcome them as well.

Rejected to Accepted

Most of us, at one time or another, have asked the age-old question, *Who am I, and why am I here?* It's the one question that has plagued man for centuries. Throughout the years, ancient philosophers and poets have carefully contemplated the meaning of life. Similarly, even modern-day musicians and artists carry on the tradition, asking questions but rarely finding true answers.

It has been said that art is a reflection of life rather than life being a reflection of art. I definitely think that this statement is true. We have all seen movie characters who spend their entire lives trying to find themselves, and I can't think of another film that more effectively embodies this statement more resoundingly than the lighthearted comedy *Runaway Bride*. In the film, the character Maggie Carpenter does not know who she is. Her extreme disconnect from herself is blatantly obvious as she makes the rounds from one relationship to the next. Her identity is wrapped up in loving and being loved, yet she doesn't even know how to love herself and keeps running from the one situation that will make her face the truth.

I do not know many people who have run away from four grooms, but I do know plenty of people who don't have a clue about their true worth and value. Maybe you are one of these people. Or you may possibly be among the few who already have a general understanding of their personal value but fall short when it comes to actually grasping that value in its entirety. Well, my aim is to help you with the unveiling process. I want to come alongside you, and let us uncover the clues together, which will help us see and understand the full picture of who we are. There is a wonderful human being beneath the surface whose contribution to this earth is powerful and truly impacting. My hope is that we will not only know our true value and worth but also that we will grab onto it with both hands.

Our Original Design

Genesis 1:26–28 says that we were created in the image and likeness of God to rule and reign on this earth. Think about the enormity of what that really means. Unlike any other species on earth, you and I were made in the image of the Creator of all things. We carry his nature on the inside of us. Housed within each of our bodies are spirits that have the ability to create, to develop, and to enhance; within us lies the capacity to love, to forgive, and to bounce back from devastating falls. Yes, within each of us are winners, not quitters, victors and not victims. These attributes are an intricate part of our spiritual DNA. These truths alone tell us that we have tremendous value. Reading further in Genesis, we see that God created us to be in relationship with him. The Bible says that Adam and Eve walked with God in the cool of the day, and until the fall of man had unhindered communication with the Maker of heaven and earth. They enjoyed his presence in their daily lives.

Despite man's fall from grace, God never lost sight of our original value and purpose, even though we as humans sometimes do. Even before mankind fell, God had a plan to reconcile us back to himself. He sent his spotless Son to save us. When Jesus went to the cross on our behalf, he restored us to the original place we have always had in our Father's heart. He also took back the authority Adam and Eve gave away to the enemy when they committed high treason in the garden. Surely we must be important if God was willing not only to fight for us but also to die for us. Do you know of a king or even a president in present or past history who was willing to die for his subjects? So why we think that the Father would be okay with us believing anything less of ourselves is beyond me.

Psalm 139:14 says that we were fearfully and wonderfully made. God formed each of us in secret and wrote all the days of our lives in his book, and from the beginning of time, God knew we would be his. As we read Ephesians 1:4–5, we discover that God picked us for himself and foreordained us to be adopted as his own children. You may find it interesting that in Old Testament times, when an heir was needed, adults were adopted. Unlike biological children, adopted children could never be written out of the will. Through our faith in Christ, we have become sons and daughters forever—children of the most high God and heirs of the King of kings. We will never be written out of his will! Never! Now, that is true value.

Sadly, as Christians who have been bought with the precious blood of Jesus, we often live so far beneath what God intended for us when we fail to see ourselves as God sees us—as valuable and precious. Jesus came to give us life, the abundant life. He wants us to have an abundance of joy, peace, love, mercy, and so much more. He has already paid the price, so we can experience this abundance in every area of our lives.

Exposing the Lies

Unfortunately, one of the reasons so few people are living the abundant life is that too many have chosen to believe the lies of the enemy over the truth. Adam and Eve did the same thing, and it led to spiritual, emotional, mental, and physical death. Like our first parents, believing a lie will cause us to forfeit an amazing destiny and future. They had no idea that the subtle bent to entertain the lies of the enemy would cost them so much, and the effects of their choice have lasted for generations.

Friends, if we haven't noticed it by now, I hope that we will open our eyes and be attentive because we do have a real enemy, and he is more of a threat than any present-day terrorist our nation has ever known. In fact, he is the father of all terror and acts of terrorism. You see, the devil is not some make-believe character in a red suit. We have to be on guard and aware of his schemes at all times.

> Your enemy the devil prowls around like a roaring lion looking for someone to devour.
>
> 1 Peter 5:8 (NIV)

Although Satan was defeated at the cross, it is up to us to enforce his defeat in our lives. If we do not stand in our rightful authority over him, he will back us into a corner with his fiery darts. Remember, the enemy's purpose is to steal, kill, and destroy; he is not content with just filling our lives up with a few minor irritations and mishaps. Friends, he plays for keeps, and from the time we were conceived, he has tried to demolish our image.

Rejection is the number-one tactic the enemy uses to rob us of our self-image. Moreover, rejection can be a major factor contributing to the slow erosion of our true selves. One of the most important truths I have discovered after nearly twenty years in ministry is that we all experience rejection at some point in our lives. From the child on the playground who is always picked last for a team, or the junior high girl who is never asked to the school dance, or the faithful employee who is passed over for yet another promotion, rejection is intricately woven into the tapestry of all our lives. Although it is very common, somehow along the way we misinterpret rejection as something personal. The message we internalize is this: *This rejection means that deep down inside I am irreparably flawed, and I don't even know it. Why else would I keep getting rejected?* When rejection comes from people we do not know well or care much about, its effects are usually minimal; however, rejection from people who are close to us can wound us deeply and alter the very core of who we are meant to be. Not being accepted by the people we love and trust, if experienced often enough, has the potential of drastically changing how we feel about ourselves as well as how we see our place in this world.

We cannot glorify God with our lives when we believe the lies that we are permanently flawed, hopeless, and have no way of breaking out of rejection's cycle. When a person passively resigns himself to accepting rejection as a way of life, he has erred greatly. Eventually, this subtle trap becomes the vehicle which welcomes mediocre mindsets that attract controllers, abusers, and manipulators into life's scene, and true to their nature, these kinds of people will only reinforce the lies. We have to be willing to see rejection in its proper perspective—as an event rather than a lifestyle. Despite our history, rejection does not have to be a permanent fixture in our lives. If, however, we believe that rejection is here to stay, that belief will undoubtedly affect our actions, and we will eventually perpetuate that same belief into our children and the generations to follow. Before we know it, we have compromised our standards to win the approval of man.

Like Maggie Carpenter, when we do not know who we really are, we then give other people and things the power to define us. It is no wonder that sooner or later we face an identity crisis. Often, we give this right to define ourselves over to a friend, a spouse, a relative, a co-worker, a job, or even a ministry. "Oh," we say. "No, they took it away from me. They demanded it," but if we look down deep inside, we have usually misplaced our value by allowing people, positions, or things to make us feel better about ourselves. I know I have been guilty of this in the past, and this false allegiance has caused me to compromise my standards in the futile attempt to win the approval of man. All that work and effort spent only to find out that I must work twice as hard to sustain that approval. The entire process is utterly and completely exhausting!

Please remember this: We set ourselves up for disappointment and rejection when we find our worth and value outside of the way God intended. The problem is that anything we place our identity in outside of God will not last. Think about moms and dads who find their identity in their children. These individuals are lost when their children grow up and move out of the house; it's called *empty nest syndrome.* The truth is that other people, positions, and things cannot make us feel better about ourselves. They may offer momentary pleasure, but they cannot fully or forever satisfy us. Ultimately, we have to see our true worth, and we can only do that if we know who we are in Christ. Christ has to be the reason we live, not our children, our spouses, or our jobs.

We All Have Needs

We all have the need to be loved, approved, accepted, and forgiven, and while everyone has the same needs, we do not always recognize the same needs. Our need for love, approval, and value is directly related to our significance and worth.

Years ago, the Lord showed me that I would never have turned to him if he had allowed anything other than himself to fill my needs. Other things can help boost our esteem, but these things can also hurt us. God has to be our source. We are like plugs designed to fit into one outlet; God is that outlet. Plugging into any other source besides God will not work. You would not expect a 220-volt plug to work if you inserted it into a 110-volt outlet; the outcome would, in fact, be shocking. God is the only place to turn to have our deepest needs met.

God knows our needs, and he wants to meet every single one of them according to his riches in glory. The place in our hearts meant only for God cannot be filled by anyone or anything else, so it remains empty, and rather than having what we require in order to operate at full power, we are just empty on the inside. Alternatives like alcohol, drugs, sex, food, and money leave painful voids in our hearts, and when we try to numb the pain or fill the voids with other substitutes, we suffer even more pain and rejection. Regrettably, few of us know that we can turn to God and be healed, so the wounds and the void just grow bigger. By the time we realize that this place in our hearts is meant only for the Lord, it has become a gaping hole the size of the Grand Canyon. The good news is that God is big enough to fill it.

I think of a time when my husband had been away on a two-week business trip. I wanted him to plan a refreshing weekend getaway for the two of us. Remembering that planning was not his strong point, I wised up and planned a quick trip myself. Everything started out wonderfully. We were having a great time at the beach until my husband picked up his fishing pole and headed toward the water. I was relaxing in the sun and can still picture the shocked expression on my face as I thought, *Where in the world is he going?* Although it may sound petty, my feelings were hurt because he wanted to fish. After all, the whole point of the trip was for us to spend time together, but he no more wanted to sunbathe than I wanted to fish. It had nothing to do with us not being together. To him, we *were* together. Instead of recognizing that we were just different, I interpreted his actions to mean that he did not want to be with me.

I was still upset that evening when we packed up and headed home. On the drive back, I heard the

Lord whisper something that set me free. He said, *You are allowing something so small to devalue you and cause rejection in your heart.* The Lord showed me that I had to take back ownership of that place in my heart because it did not belong to anyone but him. Right then and there, I blurted out to my husband, "I want it back." Of course, he had no idea what I was talking about, and with a puzzled look on his face, he asked what I wanted back. When I told him I wanted back the right to my self-worth, value, and identity, he said that he had never taken it. My precious husband had not taken the right to my identity; I had been giving it away for years.

Due to the rejection I already believed about myself, I walked around like a beggar, hoping someone would fill the empty cup, but only I could make the choice to take it back and put it into God's hands. If you are like I was, know that your spouse does not have the right to your self-worth and identity. No one but God has the right to determine your worth and value, not even you.

If we allow other people to make us feel good about ourselves, then they can also make us feel bad about ourselves. You have heard stories about domestic abuse. Maybe you have even lived one of them. A woman will stay in an abusive relationship only if she believes she is worthless. It can take years to overcome the lie of worthlessness, especially when the abuse confirms it. We must get to the point where we know who we are in Christ so that we will not allow others to treat us in ways that damage us. We can be easily moved by people's treatment if a lie is already in operation, and we have to realize that our value does not change based on how others treat us. The way we see ourselves may change, but our value in God's eyes does not. We must take the step to realize how God feels about us, how valuable and precious we are in his eyes because this will give us the courage needed to start taking responsibility for our own lives. This truth frees us to be who we are, and it also frees the people in our lives to be who they really are.

Causes of Rejection

Many things can cause rejection, including seemingly small things that might not even be true, such as the feeling that a friend is ignoring us or that a co-worker may be gossiping about us or that someone we do not even know may be looking at us in the wrong way. Other reasons for rejection are that people may refuse to accept us because of our appearance, our socioeconomic background, or our performance. Although rejection is not always intended, people's words and actions can make us feel rejected, and what might not hurt one person can wound another significantly. Words have great power to either build up or tear down, and throughout our lives, we have all had people who are more than happy to tell us who we are not. We have all had teachers, boyfriends, girlfriends, friends, and even parents who have torn us down with their words. *Sticks and stones will break my bones, but words will never hurt me* is the biggest deception that Satan ever pulled off.

The Bible tells us in Proverbs 18:21 that life and death are in the power of the tongue. The power of words is amazing. They literally chart the course of our lives because they affect the way we think and see ourselves. Words plant either good or bad seeds in the hearts of the people to whom they are spoken, and those seeds will eventually produce fruit. Kind, loving words build people up, whereas unkind, harsh words tear people down. We need to know which words spoken to us have changed us in a negative way, and we also need to be careful when speaking to others because we do not want to be the source of rejection in someone else's life.

Responses to Rejection

Although we cannot always prevent the things that cause rejection, we can choose how to respond to them. I have found that most people respond incorrectly to rejection in one of three ways and sometimes in all three. Our response to rejection is predicated on personality type.

The first response is to agree by default and keep on walking. We do this by not fighting the lie causing the rejection, and as a result, we are more likely to be deceived by the lie because we do not recognize it. Those who respond to rejection in this way usually do not realize they are allowing others to redefine them.

The second response is to agree wholeheartedly with the lie of rejection and actually reject ourselves. Basically, you are not okay with you, so you decide that you are the problem and deserve nothing less than to be rejected by others. Until they are healed, people who respond to rejection in this way are often a mess. I was one of these people and bought the lie of rejection hook, line, and sinker. Even minor incidents sent me on a downward spiral spiritually, mentally, and emotionally.

The third response, which I think is most interesting, is rebellion. A person who rebels in response to rejection thinks he should be treated like he is worth more. While that may be true, he goes about his entire life trying to prove it by doing things his way. Rebellious behavior may already be part of that individual's makeup, but it is magnified by any hurts, which cause rejection in that person's life. What a rebellious person needs, in addition to discipline, is lots of love.

Handling rejection in any one of these three ways leads to bondage. Self-protective defenses do not solve the problem; instead, they magnify it. It takes some longer to see what the lie of rejection is doing to them, but recognizing it is the first step in winning the battle. We must be aware of the words and actions that can cause rejection in our hearts. If we do not kick the seeds of rejection out immediately, the enemy will come in and try to provide circumstantial evidence that is rather convincing.

Rejection can manifest itself in many ways, depending on our personalities and our foundation of beliefs about ourselves. Shyness, anger, fear, people-pleasing, and controlling behaviors can all be evidence of rejection in a person's heart. Sometimes the overly enthusiastic and loquacious personality types are the ones who are struggling with rejection just beneath the surface. So wherever you may fall in the spectrum, it is important to your emotional and spiritual health to begin to take an honest look and to recognize the signs. A telltale sign is exhibiting great difficulty in accepting good things God says about us or even accepting a compliment from other people. Another sign is experiencing feelings of worthlessness and self-hate, constantly judging and criticizing ourselves. The more we understand how rejection works, the more clearly we recognize its operation both in others and within ourselves.

Think about the times you have been around someone you did not want to be nice to even though there was no real reason. Rejection was probably operating in that person's life. On the flipside, has that ever happened to you, detecting that others do not want to be around you for no apparent reason? The truth is that when someone believes he is rejected, he acts in ways that set him up for more rejection. The vibes he sends off can be likened to a self-fulfilling prophecy. Like quick-drying cement, his subconscious, self-defeating monologue solidifies the lie and perpetuates that cycle of rejection. People are people, and often they do not know how to behave when rejection is in operation, so they follow the path of least resistance—they treat you the way you feel about yourself, which in turn is how you expect to be treated. If you feel rejected, people will reject you. How can you expect others to accept you when you do not accept yourself? Rejection begets rejection.

The enemy's purpose in rejection is to turn our focus inward. After we have fallen for the lie, we become very selfish and self-centered. It is as if we wear a veil of mirrors on our head, and everything taking place around us bounces right back to being about us. We can walk into church and see a group of our friends talking quietly in a corner and assume they are talking about us, or we may wonder why no one calls and asks us out to lunch. That is rejection surfacing in our heart. We somehow think others should feel sorry for us because of our struggle with rejection, but the awful truth is that even if others do feel sorry for us, the diabolical nature of this spirit will cause them to pull away. In the same manner, rejection causes us to pull away from God, and God is not okay with us pulling away from him. He paid far too high a price for us not to want to come near.

For most of my life, I believed that I was rejected goods. I had experienced a lot of pain and rejection from people, and it seemed like rejection was just my lot in life. I believed that some people were luckier than others, and only the lucky ones were loved and valued. When you are as consumed with pain as I was, it is hard to imagine what it would be like to be valued and loved. Once self-pity sets in, life becomes "all about me." We cannot think about others because we are always thinking about ourselves. If we constantly hear ourselves saying the words *me*, *I*, and *mine*, it is likely that self-pity has set in.

It was never God's will for his people to be self-centered because it renders us useless in God's kingdom. One of the best ways to overcome the self-problem of rejection is to do something for someone else. Call a friend you have not talked to in a while, make a meal for your new neighbor, pray for your co-worker. Getting our eyes off of ourselves will help us to heal. I am not saying that making someone a meal will cause those deep wounds to be healed overnight. I understand that healing is a process that takes time, but I am saying that it will help advance the process by thinking of others more highly than yourself.

Years ago, God used an annual women's retreat to teach me a valuable lesson about not focusing on myself. I had attended this same retreat with the same friends each year, and this particular time, one of the ladies invited her neighbor to join us. The neighbor had a really strong personality, and because of the rejection I felt within, I assumed that she did not like me. I thought that she saw me as less valuable because that was how I saw myself; thus, most of the weekend passed without us ever talking. Toward the end of the retreat, she came up to me and told me that she thought I was one of the neatest, strongest Christian women she had ever met. I was so stunned that you could have knocked me over with a feather. I had allowed that same lie of rejection to affect the way I acted around this woman and had wasted the entire weekend not getting to know her because I was afraid of getting hurt. I thought I was protecting myself by withdrawing.

It is sad, but we all hide in some way when we think we might be rejected, which totally contradicts the way God calls us to live—loving and ministering to one another. Fortunately, God gave me the opportunity to adjust the wrong perception I had about how this woman saw me; I got a second chance to minister to someone who was just beginning to learn about God.

Rejection can cause us to miss out on life because we are so self-conscious and often feel that we are different from everyone else. Not only that, we may even feel that we are worse than everyone else and have the attitude that if people really knew us, they would reject us. When we believe the lie of rejection, we miss out on the joy, peace, and happiness God has for us. We miss out on opportunities to make a difference in other people's lives, and if we believe the lie long enough, we can miss out on our destiny.

God Accepts Us

No one is rejected! The Bible tells us that God is love and also that it is not his will that anyone perish; not even the worst of all sinners is outside of the scope of God's love. Believing in God's love changes us from thinking that we are rejected to believing that we are truly loved and accepted. Ephesians 3:18 tells us that we can experientially know the height, the breadth, the length, and the depth of God's love for us.

The truth is that every person can experience what it is like to be valued and loved no matter what they have been through. God cares about us. His love and acceptance are available to us, but we have to receive them. Jesus died on the cross for all, not just some people. He sacrificed his life so we could all come to know God as our Father. We are always welcome in his presence. He wants us to come near. God does not desire a long-distance relationship but yearns for personal intimacy with each of us. No matter what we have done or what others have done to us, God loves us.

> To the praise of the glory of his grace, wherein he hath made us accepted in the beloved.
>
> Ephesians 1:6 (KJV)

Our value never changes in God's eyes, even though it changes in our eyes. We might think God rejects us when others reject us, but that simply is not true. We should not take everything we feel at face value. Just because something feels a certain way does not make it true. I do not always feel valuable, loved, or forgiven, but that does not change the truth that I am. There are times when I have to fight feelings of worthlessness and rejection and remember that they are just feelings. We have to discern what is true; God's Word is truth. We have to learn to submit our feelings to the Spirit of God within us, and we have a choice either to believe the truth or continue believing the lies of the enemy.

In the early morning as I float in and out of sleep, negative thoughts about myself often surface in my mind. If I am not careful, I accept those thoughts and feelings just because they are familiar. I have to stop and check the validity of the thoughts running through my mind and then remind myself that Satan is the father of all lies and make a conscious decision not to allow his junk to fill my head. In times like these, I pull out my Bible and remind myself of how God sees me then tell myself what he thinks of me. Like Jesus when he was tempted by the devil, I have to fight back with the Word of God. We all do. The enemy will steal, kill, and destroy until we say, "No more." We have to actively resist. If the enemy is tap dancing on your head, tell him to shut up. Shove the Word of God down his throat.

One of our sons had to learn to stand up for himself in the battle against rejection during junior high school, which can be one of the most trying times for a young person. He was small for his age, had a high voice, and was trying to figure out who he was and what his purpose was in life. Other kids at school constantly made fun of him. When he came home from school at the end of the day, you could see the hurt all over his face. I made sure he knew I was there for him but did not push him to talk until he was ready. Eventually, he would look for me in the kitchen and tell me what happened. Not wanting to overreact, I would tell him that everyone gets made fun of because they are too short, too tall, too skinny, too fat, or their voices are too high or too low. I would tell him how awesome he was and how proud his dad and I were of him. Most importantly, I would remind him that God loved and accepted him just as he was. After all, God created him; he was unique and special. I would tell him what I am telling you.

No one has the right to make you feel bad about yourself without your permission. You get to choose whether you will allow other people's words and actions to hurt and tear you down. Our son needed what we all need from time to time; he needed to be reminded of who he truly was. Fortunately, he did not allow the teasing and hurtful words to mold him. If he had, one of his greatest talents could have been shelved and never used. His once high voice has today matured into one of the most gifted, deep singing voices I have ever heard.

Rejection starts with those things that cause us to question our self-worth, identity, and value. The enemy usually targets the gifts God has given us because they are tied to our destiny. What the enemy tries to destroy is the very thing God intends to use. God knows who we are, and he knows the plans he has for us. The enemy also knows who we are—children of almighty God—and will do anything he can to keep us from realizing this truth.

We have to learn to shake off the things that could tear us down and keep us from being who we are meant to be. We have to make a choice every time we encounter someone or something in life that causes rejection. When a snake bit the Apostle Paul, he just shook it off, and the venom did not harm him. The lie of rejection is much like a snakebite, and we have to do as Paul did and just shake it off. Rejection loses its power when we refuse to accept its poison into our hearts. Since God accepts us no matter what anyone says or does, we are still accepted.

I wasted so many years trying to fix the rejection that I wrongly believed about myself. I did not know what was dogging me, causing me to get hurt. I felt as if there was something inherently wrong with me. Other people did not seem to have the same problems in relationships that I had, which solidified the thought that there was something wrong with me. I had so agreed with the lie of rejection that it simply became who I was.

Like many, I tried to fill the need with anything that seemed to make me feel better about myself, even for a short while. In high school, I tried cheerleading, which worked until the year I did not make the team. Dating worked the same way; I felt good about myself as long as I had a boyfriend. The problem with trying to fill the void in our hearts with anything that comes along is that things change, so they can only fill the void temporarily. Only God can continually and consistently fill our hearts with everything we need. He is the only one who never changes. "Jesus Christ the same yesterday, and today, and forever" (Hebrews 13:8, KJV).

God truly loves us and wants us. He does not just tolerate or put up with us. You may have been an "oops" to your mom or dad, but you were certainly not an "oops" to God. You are not a mistake, even if your parents wanted a child of the opposite gender. If you are a girl, you were meant to be a girl. If you are a boy, you were meant to be a boy. God designed exactly what he wanted in your mother's womb. "For You did form my inward parts; You did knit me together in my mother's womb" (Psalm 139:13, AMP).

God wants to fill the role in our hearts as our Abba Father. Everything our natural parents were not, God can be to us and even more. It takes time to build our trust in this relationship, but God understands why we have trouble with trust. There has to be a time in each of our lives where we take responsibility for ourselves. At that point, we can no longer blame our behavior on the hurts of our past; we have to let go of the pain and move forward. God wants us to grow in maturity by allowing his love to heal those wounds, and receiving his love enables us to love both him and ourselves. When you really know his love, you cannot help but love others. When you are healthy and whole, you look beyond people's outward actions and simply walk in the love God requires of you. Our rejection of God's love is the only thing that can keep us from it.

> For I am persuaded, that neither death, nor life, nor angels, nor principalities, nor powers, nor things present, nor things to come, nor height, nor depth, nor any other creature, shall be able to separate us from the love of God, which is in Christ Jesus our Lord.
>
> Romans 8:38–39 (KJV)

We have a tendency to withdraw from God when we mess up, but we do not have to. "Let us therefore come boldly unto the throne of grace, that we may obtain mercy, and find grace to help in time of need" (Hebrews 4:16 KJV). While man's love is always subject to change, God's love is unconditional. It is not contingent on either our performance or the love of another human being. As we allow ourselves to believe the good news that God loves us and begin to receive that unconditional love, we then draw close to the Lord without fearing rejection. We do not have to be afraid of what he might see if we get close to him; he already sees everything and still says, *Come close.* God wants you to come near so he can tell you how awesome he thinks you are. His love is not needy, shallow, petty, or conditional, and will take you off that emotional roller coaster of life based on how others feel about you. I rode that roller coaster most of my life, and it was not fun. God's constant love set my feet on solid ground, and his love will do the same for you.

I remember when I began to know and believe God's love for myself. A friend of mine had invited me to a Christian event in someone's home, where the guest speaker practically ignored me but treated my friend like she was the most important person in the world. I soon realized that this woman was only interested in my friend because of what she could offer her. Besides that, I knew enough about rejection not to be hurt by the incident, but I did take note of the woman's behavior.

Several weeks later, I went to another Christian women's meeting, and upon arrival, I found out that the guest speaker was the same lady from the previous home group meeting. This time, she happened to overhear a conversation about what I was doing in ministry at my church. All of a sudden, I became someone worthy of her attention. She sought me out and began to talk to me. Although my human nature wanted to blow her off, I politely answered her questions. As I was forgiving her on the way back to my seat, I heard the Lord ask me if it was okay if he was the only one who noticed me when I walked into the room. Something so personal and touching happened when the Lord spoke to me, and in that moment I personally experienced the depth of God's love for me. By the time I reached my chair, I was in tears. The God of the universe—the one who put everything we see into motion—had noticed me.

God is no respecter of persons. What he has done for me, he will do for you, and he speaks personally to each one of us. We have to trust and believe that God loves us. Had I not done that, I might not have recognized his voice when he spoke to me.

I encourage you to read the book of Ephesians and mark everything that says *in Christ* and *in him*. These promises are for every born-again believer. Each of us is God's masterpiece. Nothing we do will ever cause him to reject us. "While we were yet sinners, Christ died for us" (Romans 5:8 KJV). Jesus paid our penalty so that we can have a relationship with God the Father. God wants us to believe in his goodness and love in our lives. No matter what role rejection has ever played, we can have a stable foundation based on the love of God.

I want to share something incredible from Matthew 16:13–17 (NIV):

> When Jesus came into the region of Caesarea Philippi, he asked his disciples, "Who do people say that the Son of Man is?" They replied, "Some say John the Baptist; others say Elijah; and still others, Jeremiah or one of the prophets." "But what about you?" he asked. "Who do you say I am?" Simon Peter answered, "You are the Christ, the Son of the living God." Then Jesus replied, "Blessed are you, Simon son of Jonah for this was not revealed to you by man, but by My Father in heaven."

Who does God say that you are? It does not matter what others said about us ten years ago or twenty years ago, and it does not matter what people are saying about us now. All that really matters is what God says about us. Let's receive God's love and allow him to heal our hearts. Let our Father in heaven reveal to us who we really are. Only he can do this because he created us, and he alone knows what he has put on the inside of each of us.

Let us ask the Lord to show us any rejection that might be operating in our lives. Whether the rejection is real or perceived, let's deal with it by forgiving the person or persons involved and let go of the offense and pain. Let God's truth penetrate our hearts every day, and let's believe the truth instead of the lies. Do not let the past steal another day of our lives; it has already stolen enough. Let the love of God so consume us that when the unavoidable rejections come, we will be able to walk with our heads held high, knowing that the one who knows us best loves us most and does not reject us. He is our Father God.

Dear precious Lord, forgive me for believing that I am rejected. I choose today to believe you love me, and accept me just as I am. Open my eyes to see your love for me. Amen.

From Fear to Freedom

Have you ever felt like you were different from everyone else, and because of that, you were afraid to let people really get to know you, the real you? You know what I am talking about. Not the person you let people know but the true person on the inside, the one without pretense, falsehood, or masks. In many ways, we are reluctant to reveal the real us to others because we often secretly believe that we possess some kind of grievous defect, or somehow we are a mistake.

If any of the above thought patterns mirror your current sentiments, then I too can relate. For years, the fear of being me was one of my biggest personal battles. Before I overcame this fear, I walked around like a scared little rabbit with my head down and my shoulders rolled in. It was obvious that my outward appearance was a reflection of how I felt about myself on the inside. While there was nothing truly wrong with me, I was confident that I was permanently flawed due to all the painful things that kept happening in my life. Convinced that people wouldn't like me, I began to hide my true self.

Ironically, the stories my parents tell about me are the polar opposite of what I slowly became. As a young child, I portrayed a little girl who was anything but fearful. I was not afraid of people, not even strangers, and considered everyone a friend. According to my mom and dad, I was outgoing, carefree, bold, and confident, the portrait of life. It wasn't at all unusual to see me turning cartwheels down the sidewalk, in the stores, and practically everywhere we went. I was so full of vigor. One favorite story that my parents often tell is about my zest for diving at the age of four, even before I learned how to swim! Talk about fearless! When our family vacationed each summer at Lake Walkaway in south central Mississippi, I would beg my dad to help me climb the ladder to the high diving board. Trembling with anticipation, I could hardly wait for him to get back down the ladder and into the lake so I could jump. I wasn't scared because I trusted my dad to catch me as soon as I hit the water, and can picture the sheer joy on my face and hear the excitement in my voice as I begged him to let me dive again. Dad says that I dived over and over; my unbridled energy knew no bounds. Although I had no intention of stopping, I would eventually have to since I came close to completely wearing my father out.

Slow but steady transformation from the once exuberant child revealed a completely different kind of adult. Eventually, my seemingly secure world both at home and at school crumbled. Many of the people I trusted began to let me down in some major ways, and while stinging from the pain, there were still some that deeply resented and criticized my confidence. Bit by bit, the fearlessness that marked my childhood was destroyed. Looking back, I can see how the enemy used painful circumstances and disappointments in life to prevent me from becoming the person I was meant to be.

I know now that I was not the only one battling with fear, although at times it felt that way. The truth is that everyone faces fear at some point or another. God hates fear because it causes us to flee or retreat and draw back from him. It is this presence of fear that affects the way we live our lives, how we treat other people, and ultimately hinders our ability to walk in the freedom that Christ died to give us.

We read in 2 Timothy 1:7 that fear is a spirit, and since fear causes us to focus inward, our number-one concern becomes protecting ourselves. This in turn causes us to begin withdrawing from the Lord and the people he has placed in our lives. Instead of turning to God for help in time of need, we pull away. This distance prevents us from approaching the Lord in confidence or in faith. Please remember this: We can't operate in both faith and fear at the same time. When our focus is fear, trust in God ceases. This eventually keeps us from growing and maturing spiritually.

We could spend hours talking about what we fear since there are so many phobias out there. In this chapter, I would like to focus on the fear behind all of those other fears: being afraid of God, which in turn causes us to fear being ourselves. We are not supposed to conform to some supermodel image of airbrushed perfection; God had something else in mind before we were even conceived. God purposely designed each of us with unique character traits and personalities. Yes, we are supposed to be different. Aren't you glad that God likes variety? Think how boring our relationships and lives would be if we were all the same.

According to Genesis 1:26, we are created in God's image, and it is our image or perception of God that affects how we see ourselves. When we lose sight of who God really is, we can't help but lose sight of who we are (i.e., the image of God in us). Imagine reproducing an elaborate oil painting. If your perception of the original painting is somehow flawed, the replicas you produce will also be flawed. While God is not defective in any way, our image of him sometimes is; thus, when our image of God is distorted, our image of ourselves will be distorted as well. The good news is that God sees us as we truly are, regardless of how we see ourselves, and he considers us masterpieces. "Very good," were the words of the Creator after he examined all that he had made, including man. Do the same words come to mind when you see your reflection in the mirror or hear someone call your name? Do they come to mind every time you think of yourself? If not, we can change our image of ourselves as we correct our image of God.

Painful experiences and disappointments in life are what most often tarnish our image of God, opening the door to fear. If we are afraid of God, we will also be afraid of the greatness that is intrinsically embedded within us. In other words, we will be afraid of the person God created us to be. When the Bible says to fear God, it means to respect, revere, and honor him, to be in awe of him. My goal in this chapter is to expose the lie so that we can move from fear to freedom. We are to fear (revere) God because he is holy; we do not have to be afraid of him. God is not mean, and he is not out to punish us. God is love and wants us to run to him, not from him.

Understanding Fear

Understanding fear is essential to walking in freedom. Fear is one of the primary tactics the enemy uses to steal, kill, and destroy the original design God had in mind when he created us. Fear operates in our minds, causing us to pull back from life but also causing us to pull away from others. The enemy tries to instill fear in us at a very early age, and throughout our lives, he continues to attack us with fear in an attempt to thwart the plans God has for us.

While the force of fear can be very overt, we

will discover that fear is wildly insidious. Creeping into our existence unawares, fear can be carefully absorbed into our lives through many channels—the words of a friend, a radio broadcast, or a negative seed planted by the enemy in our hearts and minds. It can exist in our lives for a long time without us recognizing it, and we can see its effects mentally, physically, and spiritually. Long before I realized that I was in bondage to fear, it had already affected me in all three ways.

Fear Affects Us Mentally

"For God has not given us a spirit of fear, but of power, and of love, and of a sound mind" (2 Timothy 1:7 NKJV). When we become fearful, we stop thinking rationally. We lose our ability to make sound decisions. Instead of making good choices based on facts or logic, we make bad choices based on fear. We react differently to circumstances when fear is controlling our minds, often withdrawing in self-protection instead of doing what we really want to. For example, fear may keep us from making new friends or talking openly to our spouse about our needs. To combat fear properly, it is imperative that we know what is going on in our thinking. Our mind is the battlefield. What goes on in our mind affects our emotions and subsequently our actions.

To win the battle against fear, we must retrain our minds with the truth of who God is and who we are to God. We are told how do this in Romans 12:2 (KJV): "And be not conformed to this world; but be ye transformed by the renewing of your mind, that ye may prove what is that good, and acceptable, and perfect, will of God." We have to make a decision that God's Word is the ultimate truth and that his Word works.

Fear Affects Us Physically

Fear can wreak havoc on our physical bodies, causing ailments such as ulcers, high blood pressure, sleep disorders, and anxiety attacks. When I was in my early thirties, I started having terrible chest pains. The pain was so intense that it took my breath away. I knew it was abnormal to have that kind of pain at my age, so I went back and forth to the doctors to find out what was wrong. After running EKGs, the doctors discovered that I had mitral valve prolapse (MVP). MVP is a common condition characterized by chest pain and an irregular heartbeat. Found mostly in women, MVP is usually not serious, and in my case, there was no cause for alarm. However, the more my chest hurt, the more stressed and fearful I became. The fear caused me to release adrenaline and tighten the muscles in my chest, increasing both the pain and my heartbeat.

I will never forget the two incidents that set me free from the vicious cycle of pain and fear. First, my doctor took the time to explain to me what was going on. Understanding is always part of the answer when there is a problem, whether mental, physical, or spiritual. The doctor told me that no one had ever died from mitral valve prolapse; then he instructed me on how to keep my heart healthy and sent me on my way. Knowing that I couldn't die from the pain immediately set me free from the fear. As my fear subsided, so did the pain. Second, a friend of mine shared how the Lord had revealed to her that the pain would go away once I beat the overwhelming fear. She was right. Once I began to conquer the fear, the pain in my chest ceased. I have not experienced any symptoms of MVP since then.

Fear Affects Us Spiritually

The Lord clearly tells us that although we are at war, we already have the victory. The battle is spiritual, and if we try to fight a spiritual battle through natural means, we will lose every time. We don't need to because the Lord assures us in 2 Corinthians 10:4 that the weapons of our warfare are not physical but mighty before God for the overthrow and destruction of strongholds. "For we wrestle not against flesh and blood, but against principalities, against powers, against the rulers of the darkness of this world, against spiritual wickedness in high places" (Ephesians 6:12 KJV).

The enemy wages war against us in order to keep us from being all that we are meant to be. Fear is one of the destructive deceits the enemy uses against us in this battle, because fear contaminates our faith and makes cowards of us. It corrodes us spiritually and causes us not to believe the power of God's Word.

Overcoming Fear

To walk in freedom, we have to exercise the spiritual authority God has given us over fear. We can't beat fear by just not being afraid. If we don't know our authority and how to use it, the enemy will beat us up. Contrary to some beliefs out there, the enemy will not leave us alone just because we decide to leave him alone. "I have given you authority to trample on snakes and scorpions and to overcome all the power of the enemy; nothing will harm you" (Luke 10:19 NIV). Although this passage is literally referring to reptiles and insects, it also has a spiritual reference. Serpents and scorpions are symbolic of the dark world of Satan's kingdom. As believers, we have been instructed to take an offensive stance against that ancient enemy of our souls. Jesus told his disciples in Mark 16:15–18 (NIV):

> Go into all the world and preach the good news to all creation. Whoever believes and is baptized will be saved, whoever does not believe will be condemned. And these signs will accompany those who believe: In my name they will drive out demons; they will speak in new tongues; they will pick up snakes with their hands; and when they drink deadly poison, it will not hurt them at all; they will place their hands on sick people, and they will get well.

These instructions still hold true for Jesus's disciples today; however, this kind of power can only be exercised in the absence of fear.

We have to be trained to fight the spiritual battles we face in this war. Can you imagine the military sending our sons and daughters to war without boot camp? We wouldn't do this in the natural, yet we do it all the time in the realm of the spirit. Just like the military, we have to be trained to recognize our enemy, his weapons, and his strategies. Our training manual for life is the Bible, and part of boot camp is reading books like this, which amplify and explain further the marvelous truths of God. We are taught how to fight spiritual battles.

> Therefore put on the full armor of God, so that when the day of evil comes, you may be able to stand your ground, and after you have done everything, to stand. Stand firm then, with the belt of truth buckled around your waist, with the breastplate of righteousness in place, and with your feet fitted with the readiness that comes from the gospel of peace. In addition to all this, take up the shield of faith, with which you can extinguish all the flaming arrows of the evil one. Take the helmet of salvation and the sword of the Spirit, which is the word of God. And pray in the Spirit on all occasions with all kinds of prayers and requests. With this in mind, be alert and always keep on praying for all the saints.
>
> Ephesians 6:10–18 (NIV)

When we understand that we are in a spiritual war and learn how to use the armor with which God has equipped us, we can win the daily battles against fear.

It is time to be honest with ourselves and assess where we might be walking in fear because to walk in victory we must engage. The Bible says in Romans 6 that we are not to allow the enemy to use our bodies as instruments of sin. In other words, we do have a choice. Will we allow Christ to use us, or will we allow the enemy to use us?

Allowing fear to control any area of your life is sin. Now, I want to make something clear. Feeling the emotion of fear is not a sin, but not doing what you know you should do because of fear is a sin. To deal with this sin, we must first ask the Lord to show us where we struggle with fear and what is at the root of this fear. God knows better than we do why we have the fears we have. He knows every unmet need, every hurtful word that was spoken to us, every painful circumstance we have been through, and every wrong choice that we have made. It is true that he knows why we are the way we are. The good news is that he still loves us, and because of his goodness, he wants to set us free from fear regardless of what caused it. God wants his children to be strong and courageous, people who do not run from what they fear but who face it head on in faith.

Faith is believing and acting on God's Word, no matter what it looks like, and a by-product of faith is courage. In order to be courageous, we have to know what the Word of God says about us. To overcome the lies of the enemy, we have to face our fear head on with the truth of God's Word. Years ago, the Lord had me write down scriptures that applied to the fear

I was facing. In addition to the obvious ones like 2 Timothy 1:7, I searched for scriptures that specifically addressed my personal fears. Since I was more determined to identify and eradicate personal fears, I was able to locate promises from the Lord that adequately addressed them with working solutions of victory. First Thessalonians 5:9 (NIV) is one of my favorite scriptures. It says, "For God did not appoint us to suffer wrath but to receive salvation through our Lord Jesus Christ." One of my greatest fears was that God was mad at me, but 1 Thessalonians 5:9 assured me that I did not need to fear God's wrath. Another life-changing scripture for me was Romans 11:32 (NIV), which says, "For God has bound all men over to disobedience so that he may have mercy on them all." This one shattered the lie that said I was the worst person on the planet. I came to realize that God is love (1 John 4:8), that he loves me as much as he loves Jesus (John 12:23), and that he was not the problem. I declared these scriptures three times a day, literally taking them as I would medicine, and I encourage you to do the same.

"My son, attend to my words; consent and submit to my sayings. Let them not depart from your sight; keep them in the center of your heart. For they are life to those who find them, healing and health to all their flesh" (Proverbs 4:20–22 AMP). Eventually, the scriptures will renew your mind, and you will start to react in faith rather than in fear. This certainly was the case in my life.

There is something that you must realize; laying the Word of God on top of the lie does not bring freedom ever! Just like we have to shut off an old tape in order to hear a new one, we have to shut off the lies in order to hear the truth. Shutting off the old, played-out recording requires being intentional and deliberate. There is absolutely no room for passivity here. We have to remove the lies so that the truth of God can penetrate our hearts, and the way to do this is to interrupt that recording of the enemy's lies by speaking out loud and declaring the truth of God's Word. You cannot fight thoughts with thoughts but with the spoken Word of God. This is a process that takes time and effort but yields wonderful results through which we are strengthened, matured, and trained for battle. Simply read the Bible and begin to study God's thoughts and God's ways of thinking, living, and acting. Do you know how Jesus was able to successfully overcome the temptation of the enemy in the desert? Even though he was extremely vulnerable to failure due to lack of food for a sustained length of time, he was able to secure victory by speaking the Word of God, and we will win the battle with fear the same way. If Jesus used the Word of God to combat the enemy, we should not be surprised that we have to do the same thing.

Fear is rooted in deception, and the enemy has been lying to God's people since the beginning of time. The problem is that we were not always able to discern the lies because they often came through the channel of well-meaning people. The enemy will use anybody and any circumstance he can to perpetuate a lie. It breaks my heart to think of all the lies I believed as a young Christian. Not only did I believe that God was angry and mean, but I thought he was playing games with me. People told me that God permitted the horrible things I went through; therefore, I could not trust God to be good based on my belief that he was okay with my being hurt and abused.

If you have faced disappointments or hurts and wondered why God did not intervene, it is possible that you may have judged God as not being good. Should this be the case, now is a good time to correct your image of God. He wants to be your Abba Father (Daddy God). The Father reveals his heart to us through the Word, and he wants us to come to him as little children. God is not mad at us. No matter how badly we mess up, he still loves us. While God hates sin, he loves the sinner. He sent his one and only Son, Jesus, to take the sins of the world upon himself and to bear our punishment. We have to understand that the exchange Christ made for us was real, and our part is to just believe and receive the benefits by faith.

The Importance of Dads

Paul spoke to Timothy as a spiritual father.

> I know that you sincerely trust the Lord, for you have the faith of your mother Eunice and your grandmother Lois. This is why I remind you to fan into flame the spiritual gift God gave you

when I laid my hands on you. For God hasn't given you a spirit of fear and timidity, but of power, love and self-discipline.

2 Timothy 1:5–7 (NLT)

What I find interesting in this passage is that there is no mention of a dad or granddad. Paul's admonition implies that Timothy might be lacking in confidence because his father did not feed his faith. You might be wondering why that matters. It is primarily our dad's job to build our confidence and show us our value. We need our dad to pick us up, put us on his lap, and tell us how wonderful we are and how great we can be. Dads teach their children by example how to have faith. In essence, Paul was saying to Timothy, "You can go out and do what God has called you to do. Son, you can succeed!"

I remember talking with a woman about some problems she was having with her young son. We discovered that the root of the problem was an absent father. The boy's father was a good man, but although he loved his family, they often came second. His work was always first. The father spent very little one-on-one time with his son and assumed his son was doing fine. After all, he had a nice home, food, clothing, the latest toys, and a mother who was very involved in his life.

As a mother myself, I like to think that moms make a huge impact on their children, and although I honestly believe we do, our impact does not compare to that of a father. I believe that is part of the reason the enemy has worked overtime to break up homes and cause fathers not to be involved in their children's lives. One of the best things a dad can do for his children is to love their mom. Children are more secure when raised by parents who love each other. Unfortunately, many dads are not filled with truth and confidence themselves and can only teach their children what they have learned. Regrettably, the art of fathering has been lost due to divorce, abuse, and adultery that have torn the traditional family apart. Studies have actually shown that the children of divorced parents who were raised by a loving, godly father did better than those children who were raised by a loving, godly mother.

Please understand that I am not in any way minimizing a mom's contribution to a child's life, just simply stressing the significance of dads. Our relationship with our natural father is so important because it shapes how we see God. How we see our dads will directly affect our image of God as Father. What is your image of your dad?

Do you withdraw from him in fear when you do something wrong, or do you run to him for forgiveness? Is it easy for you to snuggle up close in his arms, or do you approach him carefully with your scorecard in hand? It might surprise you to see that you respond to your heavenly Father much like you do to your natural father. The more shattered your father image is, the greater your tendency is for fear. And if you were not fathered correctly, you won't have the confidence to live life boldly and without fear. Even the best earthly dads, in all their love and affection, do not portray God perfectly. God is the only perfect Father.

Okay, so maybe your dad didn't do his job. Your job is to forgive him for whatever he did or didn't do. You must let go of the hurts and allow the Lord to heal your heart. David writes in Psalm 68:5 (AMP), "A father of the fatherless and a judge and protector of the widows is God in His Holy habitation," and while people can have a natural dad, they can still be considered fatherless.

Allow God to meet every need that has gone unfulfilled in your life. There isn't a person on the planet who isn't in need of the heavenly Father, and regardless of what our relationship was like with our earthly dads, we are still susceptible to hurts that need a healer. God can meet your need for a father and heal any broken place in your heart. He has healed my heart and been everything to me a father should be. God is no respecter of persons. What he has done for me, he will do for you.

Coming to Know Abba Father

Years ago, I attended a women's retreat at Brookhill Ranch, Hot Springs, Arkansas, where I learned the truth about my relationship with our heavenly Father that changed my life. My friends and I loved going to these retreats in Arkansas because we always left with some part of our hearts touched and healed. Although I was seeking healing and trying to learn more about God and his ways, beneath the surface, in the deepest part of my heart, I kept some hurts at bay. Maintaining a careful distance, I was reluctant to be truthful about my pain with my heavenly Father. The theme of the retreat that weekend was Jesus revealing the Father. The truth that the Lord spoke to me was that I simply did not trust him. He showed me that I saw the Father as this angry guy in the sky from whom Jesus had to protect me.

It changed how I saw God. John 8:28 tells us that Jesus did only what the Father told him to do. What Jesus did while he was on this earth came directly from the heart of God. That truth alone should change our image of God, for while Jesus was tough, he was never mean. He told the truth but always with kindness and mercy.

I love the story about the woman who had been caught in adultery. When she was brought before Jesus, he stooped down, started writing in the sand, and said to her accusers to let whoever was without sin among them be the first to throw a stone at her (John 8:7). Well, no one stuck around to throw any stones. With the hypocrisy of their hearts being revealed, each man walked away deeply convicted of his own error and secret sins. Then, just like a loving but firm savior, Jesus said to her (John 8:11 NKJV), "Neither do I condemn you. Go and sin no more." He did not raise his voice, slap her in the face, or openly insult her. Instead, Jesus showed compassion and mercy toward her by forgiving her. I can only imagine the look in his eyes as he spoke to her with a look of authority, filled with love. I believe it changed her forever. One look from Jesus will change you too!

Everywhere in the gospels you can see the Father's heart clearly revealed by the way Jesus treated people. The only people he got angry with were the religious leaders who kept putting laws on the people, laws that were impossible to fulfill. As you read through the New Testament, you will find that Jesus forgave sins, cast out demons, and healed the sick. Like the Father, Jesus was compassionate, merciful, and full of love, and it is love in action that moved and still moves him to reach down deep into the human heart and minister healing to the wounds created by fear. He is ready and able to turn a heart of stone into a heart of flesh (Ezekiel 11:19). In my personal journey, I finally came to a place where I could begin to see the Father's heart revealed through Jesus, and with that newfound revelation, fear and lack of trust diminished and eventually left.

> There is no fear in love; but perfect loves casts out fear, because fear has to do with punishment; and the one who fears is not perfected in love.
>
> 1 John 4:18 (NASB)

While we may not love God perfectly, his love for us is always perfect. God's love is the only perfect love we will ever experience. It is not manipulative, mean, selfish, or conditional. His unconditional love is amazing. No matter what we do, right or wrong, God loves us. Unlike the love of people, God's love for us never changes. The love of the Father is pure and undefiled, and when we understand God's love, the stronghold of fear comes crashing down.

Love has to be received in order for it to be effective, and as simple as that statement is, many of us find ourselves stumbling over this basic truth. For some odd reason, we forget our role in this grand love relationship with the Father. It requires both giving and receiving from all. Now, the Father doesn't have any problem giving of his love extravagantly; the issue is with our receiving it. "We love him, because he first loved us" (1 John 4:19 KJV).

As we learn more about God and grow in our relationship with him, our love for him will grow. To see God as he really is has given me great peace and the ability to trust him. Now I can go through life with the confidence that I am chosen, forgiven, and loved by the Creator of the universe. God loving me so personally has changed every relationship in my life. Isn't it interesting the parallel between our love for God and our love for people? When a person truly embraces the heart of God, he can in turn embrace people. The more I learn of his love, the more I love him back. When I let God love me, I can love others in return.

Let me challenge you in something. Allow God the chance to heal your image of him. True healing can only take place when we come to know the Father's love for us. Once we experience his love for us, we will be able to love ourselves as well as our neighbors. Our image of God is reflected in how we treat others. If we think God is a harsh taskmaster waiting to punish us, we are likely to be harsh and unforgiving toward others, including ourselves.

When we see God as a loving, forgiving, and merciful Father, we can extend that same love, forgiveness, and mercy both to ourselves and to others.

Even if you were not raised with the truth, you can become confident in the love of God. The only way to be free from fear is to accept the Father's love and begin to trust him. Trust is defined as the assured reliance on the character, ability, strength, or truth of someone or something. We place our confidence in the one we trust. Ultimately, fear is a lack of trust in God. If you are experiencing that kind of distrust toward the Lord, I want to encourage you to allow him to teach you how to trust him. He alone knows what it is going to take. There is no magic formula for learning to trust God; we have to come to know him through prayer, worship, and the study of his Word. Don't get caught up in religious acts. Just go and spend quality time with God. Ask him how to trust, and he will show you.

We must humble ourselves to trust God. Only when we shift our trust from strongholds of the self-protective ways we have relied on for so long, can we place real trust in God. We cannot trust God without faith. Faith is assurance in God's character even when we can't see it based on our circumstances. As we come to know God more, we can choose to trust him and have faith even when we don't understand because it is easier to trust someone when we know that his intentions toward us are good. As we come to know the greatness of the God who created the universe and set the world in motion, we learn to trust him to take care of our children, meet our needs, and fulfill his purpose in our lives. We can even learn to trust him enough to tell us whom we can and can't trust. We must accept the love he offers and allow it to fill those places in our hearts that have been occupied by fear and distrust. Love is the one sure thing that will change our hearts, and God is love. It's okay to draw near to your heavenly Father. You are always safe in his arms, and in his arms you are free to be you.

Free to Be You

Fear is designed to keep us from being who we were created to be and to keep us from being bold and confident enough to do what God has called us to do. Remember, the enemy's purpose is to steal, kill, and destroy. Fear steals our trust, and without trust, we won't step out in faith. Fear beats us up so we can't possibly stand and glorify God. It can be hard to believe Jeremiah 29:11 when we've been knocked down so much. But it's never too late to agree with the vision God has always had for you. We must be bold, brave, and courageous in order to fulfill our purpose and be effective in the kingdom of God.

God's purpose is to restore us to his original design for us. He promises to restore to us more than the enemy has ever stolen. It is thrilling for me to see individuals I have ministered to break free from fear. I see them singing in the choir, teaching the Word of God, and pursuing dreams they would otherwise never have pursued. It took twenty-five years for the

Lord to completely deliver me from fear, and today I'm not afraid to be honest with myself and with God about my faults and weaknesses. I can be honest because I'm no longer afraid of rejection. I know that God is going to love me no matter what, and I've learned over time to accept myself. I am secure in who I am in Christ and am no longer moved by what others think of me. How other people treat me does not determine my value. The fearlessness I had as a child has returned. As an adult, I also have discretion that I didn't have as a child and can therefore make decisions regarding potential relationships and opportunities based upon wisdom and discernment. I am able to fly and do things I've always wanted to do because I trust that God has me in the palm of his hand. If there is something I shouldn't do, I trust him to warn me. Now, it doesn't have to take you twenty-five years to be free from fear; God wants his people well now.

God can deliver you from the fear of being yourself. Ask the Lord to show you who you were before the pain and disappointments of life changed your personality. He will show you and promises to restore you to the way you were in the beginning. He has done it for me, and I have watched him do it for others. Ask God what your fears are. Forgive your parents for whatever they may have done to hurt or mar your self-image. Remember, they could only give what they had. It is most likely that your parents did not have anyone building them up with affirming, life-giving words. Additionally, forgive anyone else who has caused mistrust within your life, and after you forgive, be sure to let those things go. Continue to reject any lies others have told you about yourself or about God. Finally, begin to believe in God's love for you. When you do this, you will move from fear to true freedom, and that is what I pray for you.

Dear precious Lord, knowing God is what heals fear. I choose to seek you because I know that as I do, you will deliver me from all my fears. Amen.

From Doubt to Determined Faith

Faith is one of the most important aspects of finding and keeping freedom. Without this critical spiritual weapon in our arsenal of support, we will find ourselves severely lacking. While this spiritual element can be used to attain and to secure the earthly needs we humans all share, our focus goes beyond the attainment of material goods but rather to wholeness and freedom from the past. Ours is a discussion of the God kind of faith, the type of faith that tenaciously believes God for the impossible and takes him at his Word. While there are times when we sincerely think we have faith, the true test of unwavering faith occurs when something bad happens. If our response to difficulty and trial is that we run back to doubt, then we are only revealing that we have allowed our experiences to program us to lend out minds and hearts to doubt rather than trust. Many of our interactions with others have trained us to expect people to be untrustworthy, so consequently we transfer that same distrust and suspicion to God, who is always trustworthy. Sadly, there are people who call themselves Christians but have no idea how to trust and believe God.

Faith to be Free

God wants you to be free, but if you do not believe that, you will not walk in this truth. We all use a form of faith every day. We have faith that we will wake up each morning and that our car will get us where we need to go, but the faith I am talking about is heart faith. Heart faith is faith in the integrity of God's character that is spoken of in the Bible. Life is going to happen; therefore, without a solid belief system we will always waver when trials come and then wrongly interpret the trial as punishment or abandonment from the Lord. As long as I had inaccurate beliefs concerning God, the same things continuously snared me. The minute something bad happened, I would doubt God and his goodness.

Doubt can be one of the hardest strongholds to overcome because often circumstances scream at us, telling us we should not believe. I am convinced that doubt is at the root of most problems in our walk with the Lord. If we really knew the Word and believed it, we would find ourselves living in complete victory. Even though many of our experiences make it easier not to believe God, the God I've come to know is totally trustworthy and can be believed.

Hebrews 11, the famous hall of faith chapter, is a discourse that heralds the lives of ordinary people with extraordinary faith. These were individuals who were strong in battle, shut the mouths of lions, and escaped death. Others in this same chapter were mocked, stoned, or killed, but no matter what they went through, they continued in faith. What I find interesting is that they found favor with God because of their faith, not because of their performance. Often, we put our faith in our own performance to keep us out of trouble rather than having faith in God's goodness to protect us.

God is a good God who wants to heal and restore his children. My aim is to assist you in building your faith to believe that God loves you and has good things in store for you. In Jeremiah 29:11 (AMP), it says, "For I know the thoughts and plans that I have for you, says the Lord, thoughts and plans for welfare and peace and not for evil; to give you hope in your final outcome."

Believing starts with choosing. Ephesians 4:22–24 (NLT) says:

> Throw off your old evil nature and your former way of life, which is corrupted by lust and deception. Instead, let the Spirit renew your thoughts and attitudes. Put on your new nature, created to be like God—truly righteous and holy.

We have been made new through Christ Jesus. We have a choice. Instead of operating on autopilot and allowing our fears to shape our thoughts, we can rely on the Word through our renewed minds to help us know and identify the truth. We can choose to believe that we are not bound by what has happened to us nor by the poor choices we have made. This scripture says that if we are in Christ, we are now righteous, holy, and true. Many people feel that those words are not true all the time, but they are. That is why we are to choose to believe the good things in the Bible about God and the way he sees us every time our feelings tell us differently. We must also believe these good things when others tell us differently.

Jesus Made a Way

The key to believing those good things is to understand the exchange Christ made for us. Christ's sacrificial offering of his own life satisfied the payment required for sin. This exchange, however, will not benefit us if we do not understand what it accomplished. Since we are totally forgiven, we do not have to fear God's punishment. The cross made us brand new and complete in Christ so that God can accept us. When Jesus cried out from the cross, "It is finished," in John 19:30 (KJV), he was letting mankind know that the price had been paid in full and that we are now totally free from all condemnation. When God looks at us, he sees us as completely righteous in him. It takes faith and humility to walk in this truth.

I spent years of my Christian life thinking I could somehow earn something from God. Failure was my constant companion. At times, I would perform well, and at other times, I would fail miserably. This inconsistency caused me to feel condemned. Finally, after another long talk with my sister, I received the truth that she spoke to me. She had patiently put up with my tears of condemnation for weeks on the phone. She truthfully stated that it was not about me.

The gospel, or good news as we know it, is that the hard part has all been done for us. We don't have to earn our righteousness. Instead, it was purchased for us through Jesus' death, burial, and resurrection. We have been made righteous; there was nothing we could do to earn it. We have to humble ourselves and admit that we cannot measure up, not even on our best days. Pride makes us think that we should be able to do better on our own and that we do not need any help. Unfortunately, pride is usually what gets in the way. When I chose to humble myself, I believed that God loved me and that he was not mad at me. On our best and worst days, we deserve hell. Fortunately, God's grace and mercy are so infinite that all we have to do is believe. Truly, that is the good news!

We do not deserve anything from the Lord. We are called to believe, and in believing, we will find that we act better because we believe better about ourselves. Our performance has nothing to do with God's love for us; he loves us in spite of how we act. God hates sin, but he loves people. We misunderstand the grace of God when we think we have to earn our way to him. We are not going to be perfect until the day we get to heaven. This is not a license to sin; it just gives us freedom to be people. My walk with the Lord remains steady as long as I remember that I am forgiven and loved based on what Jesus has done, not what I do.

Catching the Thief

In John 10:10 (NASB), it says, "The thief comes only to steal, and kill and destroy; I came that they may have life, and have it abundantly." The word for *life* in this passage is *zoë*, God's kind of life on this earth. What can be more abundant than believing and walking in the love God has for us instead of all the unkind things we have been told? Before I realized that I had to use my faith to overcome my past, I was consistently tarred and feathered by the lies of the enemy. As children, we do not recognize when someone is attaching a lie to our souls. Naively, we allow the lie to attach itself to the way we see ourselves, which gives the thief a chance to steal a part of who we are meant to be.

As we grow into adulthood, life can become an emotional roller coaster ride. I was on one of those roller coasters for some time. My ups and downs determined which way I went and what I believed. The garbage I believed about myself and about God kept me from finding the truth, even in the Bible. I would read the same passages as other people and feel just as bad as I had before I read them. While I would get excited about the things I was learning, at the first sign of trouble, I would go back to doubting; faith was the missing ingredient in my life.

I needed faith to believe that the wonderful things I was learning from my studies of the Bible applied personally to me. For some reason, many of us have a hard time with that. It's easier to believe for someone else than for ourselves. We can believe that God wants to be good to those we think are super-spiritual or more Christlike than we are, but allow me to set you free by exposing that lie. God wants to be good to each and every person on this earth. Unfortunately, there are those who do not take him up on his offer. "The Lord is not slow in keeping his promise, as some would understand slowness. He is patient with you, not wanting anyone to perish, but everyone to come to repentance". (2 Peter 3:9 NIV)

The Lord wants to heal our hearts so we can know our identities in Christ. He wants us to know what he thinks of us so we can be grounded in his love. As we become grounded in his love, we know that he is always for us, no matter what life throws our way. No matter what area in your life requires healing, it will take faith to grasp the truth from your heart to your head. Let me give you a tip: wholeness takes work. It requires putting the truth in your head through reading, studying, praying, and listening to sound, Bible-based messages. I used to think that those things kept me in right standing with God, but being in right standing with God is not based on our actions. It is based only on what Christ did for us on the cross, and its impact on our lives becomes a personal reality when we dare to believe and embrace it.

When bad experiences take place, if we are not careful, we can allow confusion to enter our hearts concerning God's character and his intentions toward us. "I have told you these things, so that in me you may have peace. In this world you will have trouble. But take heart! I have overcome the world" (John 16:33 NIV). Jesus is telling us clearly that life happens, but it does not have to destroy our faith, because he overcame those things.

We have to remember that we live in a sin-filled world full of sin-filled people—not to mention an archenemy. While we cannot coerce anyone to do right, our job is to take responsibility for ourselves and the way we live. We cannot change anyone else, but we can allow God to change us. I spent years blaming God for the way people treated me. Unfortunately, I never stopped to look at what *I* could change. We have to leave other people to God. Some things happen in our lives because of sin, be it our choices or others' choices, and we also live in a world where we cannot control everything that happens.

At other times, we might find ourselves under the attack of the enemy. We call him Satan or the devil. He has been playing games with people for longer than we have been alive. In Genesis 3:1–5 (NLT), it says:

> The serpent was the shrewdest of all the wild animals the Lord God had made. One day he asked the woman. "Did God really say you must not eat

the fruit from any of the trees in the garden?" "Of course we may eat fruit from the trees in the garden," the woman replied. "It's only the fruit from the tree in the middle of the garden that we are not allowed to eat. God said, 'You must not eat it or even touch it; if you do, you will die.'" "You won't die," the serpent replied to the woman. "God knows that your eyes will be opened as soon as you eat it, and you will be like God, knowing both good and evil."

Look closely at what the enemy was doing through the serpent. He convinced Eve that God was not good and that he was holding out on her. He wanted her to exalt herself above God just like he did before he was kicked out of heaven. Satan was tempting her to believe that she could be just like God. The sad part of this story is that Adam and Eve were as much like God as they could be. They had been created in his image and were living in perfection. Adam and Eve were walking with God in this paradise. As you may recall the rest of the story, Eve believed the lie, ate of the tree, and gave some to her husband. This one act brought death—not just a natural death but also spiritual death for them and all mankind.

You see, the enemy has been doing the same thing in the hearts of man since the beginning of time. If he can cause us to believe that God is not good and is holding out on us, we will never walk in the faith and truth we are supposed to.

You might notice that in the scriptures, it says

that he came as the shrewdest of all creatures. So it is in our lives; he comes in subtle, cunning, and sneaky ways. The enemy has no new tricks. He plants seeds of doubt in our hearts about God and his character, and we become captive to those thoughts.

> Casting down imaginations, and every high thing that exalteth itself against the knowledge of God, and bringing into captivity every thought to the obedience of Christ.
>
> 2 Corinthians 10:5 (KJV)

We must understand that the place where we have to engage in battle is in our minds. We are three-part beings: spirit, soul, and body. Ephesians 4:30 tells us our spirits have been sealed with the promise of the Holy Spirit. I believe this means that this part of us has been brought to life by believing the good news and is sealed and off limits to the enemy.

Our souls are made up of our mind, will, and emotions, and since they have not been sealed, we are called to work out our salvation daily, according to Philippians 2:12. The enemy attacks God's children through our souls, the part of us that is not redeemed. The lies that have been planted in our souls give the enemy an inroad to harass us. Once the truth is exposed in a certain area of our lives, the lie has no more authority over us, and we are set free. "Then you will know the truth, and the truth will set you free" (John 8:32, NIV).

From our earliest days, the enemy has bombarded us with questions with the intention of causing us to doubt God; questions like, *Who is this God? Did God really promise you that?* or *If God is so good, why did he let that horrible thing happen in your life?* His biggest lie is, *Can you really trust him?* We all hear those thoughts in our minds. The bottom line is that the enemy wants you to doubt God and his goodness, but it is important for you to remember, "When he lies, he speaks his native language, for he is a liar and the father of lies" (John 8:44 NIV).

When we recognize that he has been lying to us all these years, we can begin to renew our minds and purge our thinking of his tainted thoughts. We can acknowledge that we have doubted God and then allow our heavenly Father to heal and restore our image of him.

Choose to Believe

But Christ (the Messiah) was faithful over His [own Father's] house as a Son [and Master of it]. And it is we who are [now members] of this house, if we hold fast and firm to the end our joyful and exultant confidence and sense of triumph in our hope [in Christ]. Therefore, as the Holy Spirit says: Today, if you will hear His voice, do not harden your hearts, as [happened] in the rebellion [of Israel] and their provocation and embitterment [of Me] in the day of testing in the wilderness. Where your fathers tried [My patience] and tested [My forbearance] and found I stood their test, and they saw My works for forty years. And so I was provoked (displeased and sorely grieved)

with that generation, and said, They always err
and are led astray in their hearts, and they have
not perceived or recognized My ways and become
progressively better and more experimentally
and intimately acquainted with them. Accord-
ingly, I swore in My wrath and indignation, they
shall not enter into My rest. [Therefore beware]
brethren, take care, lest there be in any one of
you a wicked, unbelieving heart, [which refuses
to cleave to, trust in, and rely on [Him] leading
you to turn away and desert or stand aloof from
the living God.

Hebrews 3:6–12 (AMP)

This scripture says that our unbelief will cause
us to turn away and stand back from God. That is
exactly what we do when we are in doubt. We pull
away from God by not spending time with him or
by not reading the Bible quite as often. We pull our
hearts away. Despite this tendency, we have to get
smarter than that. If you find yourself not getting
close to the Lord or your relationship with him is
not going well, evaluate yourself to see if you are in
doubt and unbelief. It really can be that simple. If so,
the good news is that we can do something about it.

Continuing on in Hebrews 3:19 (AMP), it says,
"So we see that they were not able to enter [into His
rest], because of their unwillingness to adhere to and
trust in and rely on God [unbelief had shut them
out]." Here we see that doubt coupled with unbelief
will shut us down and shut us out of the good provision he has in store for us. This is the very reason

God calls any form of unbelief wicked. He calls it thus because it slams the door shut on all that he has for you. When you recognize unbelief in your life, own up to it and move on into faith. Do not allow unbelief to cut off your access to God's blessings. Just stay in the fight and do not give up.

The rest that God wants for his children is the true rest in our hearts and souls. This rest is something worth fighting for. True rest means we trust God. Resting means we have ceased striving, and we believe that God has us in the palm of his hand. We can rest when we know that he is good and has planned well for his children.

It is time to take inventory. What do you believe about God? What do you specifically believe God for today? What do you believe God thinks of you? If you find unbelief in any of these areas, you will not be able to walk in faith and trust. Without faith and trust, there will be no rest in your soul. If we really understood how much God loves us, we would walk this life out with confidence and boldness. When we believe that we are special to God, we can walk with our heads held high, no matter what has previously happened to us.

Jesus died so that we could be in relationship with the Father. We are called to believe in what Jesus accomplished for us on the cross and appropriate that into our lives today. Without faith, we will not be able to walk out our destinies the way we are supposed to. As we come to know the truths that set us free, we are to share those truths with others. We have been called with purpose for the purposes of God.

Faith and presumption are two different things. Be wary of presumption. We should make sure we know God's Word and his promises to us in order to keep from presuming. Our faith is set up for failure when we presume. Faith says, *I believe in God, his character, and his promises.* Presumption tells God how to do what we have asked of him. I used to presume that God would answer every prayer just the way I prayed them. I learned the hard way that God is going to do what is best for me even when I ask for something else because he is God and I am not. That is his goodness. We must let God administer his plans for our lives because his ways are best for us.

Romans 12:3 tells us that we have all been given the measure of faith. Faith will not grow if it is not used. I have always thought of faith as a muscle. If you want it to work and be useful, you must build it up. God has granted each of us the measure of faith, but what we do with it is up to us. "And without faith it is impossible to please God, because anyone who comes to him must believe that he exists and that he rewards those who earnestly seek him." (Hebrews 11:6 NIV). Our part is to believe. We must believe to be saved, and we must continue believing to stay free. Each day, we are faced with the choice of whether to believe or not believe. It is our choice. Are you going to believe when life gets tough? Are you going to believe when nothing makes sense? It helps to know what causes you to doubt because then you can arm yourself with the truth before your faith takes a hit.

Romans 4:13 (NLT) states, "Clearly, God's promise to give the whole earth to Abraham and his descendants was based not on his obedience to God's law, but on a right relationship with God that comes by faith." Abraham was a mighty man of God who is known for his acts of obedience to God. One of the amazing things about this remarkable man was his willingness to do some tough things that were required of him. Yet it was his faith that was accounted to him as righteousness. Likewise, our faith is accounted to us as righteousness. As we take an active stance on the Word to deliberately believe God as Abraham did, we too will begin to realize all that the Lord has called us to be. Rather than continue down the path that believes the lies of the enemy and then in turn be unsuccessful, choose to agree with God. By believing God, we can walk in faith and trust the one who knows us best and loves us most!

Dear precious Lord, I choose to believe that I am in right standing with you based solely on what Jesus accomplished for me on the cross. Amen.

From Insecurity to Proper Responsibility

Before I learned to really trust God, I was a card-carrying member of two distinctly opposing camps. Odd as it might sound, I frequently wove in and out of the camps of the controlled and the controller. While the camps would appear to be polar opposites of one another, and while one camp emulates victimization and the other that of an oppressor, in actuality, these two camps share a unique common denominator. A carefully woven thread runs through them both. The common denominator that both these camps share is a misplaced trust.

Interestingly, while many people can attest to being controlled, fewer recognize their own tendency to control others. The reality is that we all try to control someone or something to one degree or another. Like the ring of power so potently portrayed in the Oscar-winning film trilogy *The Lord of the Rings*, control wields a tremendous power both to enslave and to be enslaved. While a controller starts off wearing control, before long, control is wearing him.

What is this fascination with control? In Genesis 1:28 (KJV), we find that God gave man the command to dominate: "Let us make man in Our image, after Our likeness; and let them have dominion." Dominion over what? The passage goes on to state, "And let them have dominion over the fish of the sea, and over the fowl of the air, and over the cattle, and over all the earth, and over every creeping thing that creepeth upon the earth." God placed within man the intrinsic capacity to dominate and to lead, but notice, please, that nowhere does it state that man is to have dominion over another man. However, due to his fall from grace, man's innate design became corrupt, and instead of dominating the animals and the earth to cause it to yield and produce, man began to impose his will and dominate one another. This was not what the Father intended. Additionally, man's yearning for power often directed him to embrace a philosophy of self-sufficiency. Sadly, in his own eyes, he became his own god. The more he fostered a trust within himself and within his own ability, he diminished his trust in God Almighty.

We all have needs, and the thirst to quench these insatiable needs in our lives drives us to grasp at the wheel again. Yes, we take control when we try to meet our own needs rather than allowing God to meet our needs.

While control is fueled by self-sufficiency, it is interesting to note that nearly all forms of control find their root in the sticky mire of insecurity. If we feel uncertain or void of confidence, then we will inevitably either succumb to the will of another or opt to impose our will upon another. A more appropriate response to these feelings of uncertainty would be to take the plunge of surrender with face lifted toward the sky, arms fully extended, and a heart set upon sweet release. The picture I am trying to describe is similar to the old Nestle tea commercial. Just let go and fall into the arms of God. It is in that moment when your heels are hanging over the edge of the cliff and you feel the natural tendency to resist, to hang on a little longer to the familiar, and to contemplate whether you should take the dive that you have to trust and just do it. Just let go. True security is found in Christ alone. Contrary to the endless barrage of logical thought, the security that you seek is over the edge—when your will becomes his will and his alone.

When we allow others to control us, this serves as a clear signal that we do not esteem ourselves as God does. In other words, we are not confident in who he made us to be. We must remember this: God created us in his image, and the result of that wondrous design is a unique personality all our own. Our self-image influences how we relate to others as well as how we react to situations. A low self-image will prevent us from fulfilling our destiny and doing the necessary functions that God has specifically called us to.

God calls all of us, first and foremost, to love him. Second, he calls us to love our neighbor as ourselves (Matthew 22:37–39). Love is the fuel of God's kingdom; nothing works without it. We can't forgive, show mercy, or serve unless we love. 1 John 5:3 says we show our love for God by obeying his commands. We love because God first loved us (1 John 4:19); however, we can only love to the degree that we receive God's love. It is much easier to receive the love God has for us when we are secure in him and in who he created us to be.

Most people who control others are not evil; their self-absorption and preoccupation with *I* is a key indicator that they have not completely relinquished their desire to have their own way. They are of the mindset that their way is the only right way. First Corinthians 13:5 says love does not demand its own way, but the spirit of control does. Control is all about *me* and *my way*. It is the epitome of selfishness, and its anthem is the total and complete drive to look out for number one.

Methods of Control

Control manifests differently depending on the individual. One person may yell to get someone to do things his way; another person may cry. Anger, intimidation, dominance, possessiveness, and manipulation are common methods people use to control others. Now, although boldness and organization are definitely necessary gifts that God has given to his children, if these gifts are not submitted to the Lord, these too can easily turn into forms of control.

Anger

Anger is the most common vehicle of control. There is no mistaking it. When controllers become angry or irate, they often yell and scream; however, anger doesn't always relay itself in volatile expressions. There are other subtle and covert tactics that anger uses to emit its flames. Does the silent treatment sound familiar? How about stonewalling, emotional or physical withdrawal, and/or absence? Angry controllers are always emotionally abusive even if they are not physically abusive; however, in extreme cases, anger can escalate to physical abuse. Emotional abuse is as destructive and painful as physical abuse.

The price for not doing things the way of the controller is always high when anger is involved. The minute that person feels out of control, he begins to get angry and lash out, hurting others with his words and actions. Unfortunately, I have been an eyewitness to such behavior and can testify firsthand to the damage caused by anger. Before I began to walk out the truth of the Word in this area of my life, I was held at bay by a number of individuals whose explosive anger controlled me. Regrettably, I allowed their angry domination to cause me to cower in fear and shame, resulting in the total rejection of my otherwise bold and confident personality. Fearful of rocking the boat, I would clam up, keeping my thoughts and opinions bottled inside. This habit found its way into my ministry. I couldn't even counsel effectively because I was always anticipating the client's anger. Had the Lord not freed and restored me from control and its damaging effects, I doubt that I would be fulfilling my call in ministry today.

Intimidation

Intimidation is not as readily perceived as anger, but it is just as destructive. Someone who controls by intimidation may use threats, insults, or aggressive behavior to frighten another person into submission. Generally, controllers who do not wish to be confronted or questioned develop behavior that intimidates others, and with the intimidation is a clarion message underscored in no uncertain terms that says, *Don't mess with me. If you do, you'll pay.* Bullies are perfect examples of individuals who control others with intimidation. They may appear big and mean on the outside, but they are weak and cowardly on the inside.

Dominance

Most controlling people use a degree of dominance to get their way. I am not referring to someone who just has a strong (dominant) personality. You can have a strong personality and still love others by helping them become their best. In fact, every relationship will have one individual with a stronger personality, and that's okay. It's actually a good thing. While different personalities complement each other, a problem arises when the individual with the stronger personality puts the other person down or causes him or her to feel less important.

Dominance as a form of control commands or prevails over others. Someone who controls with dominance tells others where to go, what to do, and how to do it. Dominant controllers keep others under their thumb by keeping them in a place of need—for example, the need of guidance, instruction, or assistance, especially in decision making.

Possessiveness

Possessiveness is a form of control that stems from a desire to own or dominate. Many marriages fall apart because the women are treated like their husbands' possessions. In other words, he likes the way she looks on his arm, but he doesn't spend time relating to her.

A possession is something we own, not a relationship we have. For example, I own a car. I drive it wherever I want it to go, and I am in charge of my car; the car is my possession. A relationship is not a piece of property or something we own; it is a connection we have with another person. Genuine relationships should have consistent ebbs and flows, a balance between give and take, but certainly not control.

The problem with treating people like property is that they begin to lose themselves. A person loses his unique individuality, purpose, and hope upon falling under the grip of ownership. When ruled by a possessive personality, we forfeit our abilities to mature into the people we are supposed to be.

Manipulation

Manipulation is the most insidious and the subtlest form of control. The person being manipulated is often unaware of what's happening. Women are notorious for using manipulation to get their way. We have all heard the stories about women who shed tears, display extreme emotions, or withhold sex to get their way with their husbands. That is not to say that men never manipulate or that all women do. It is just that controlling women tend to use this tactic more readily than men. Other examples of manipulation include guilt trips, whining, and complaining.

A parent can put a child on a guilt trip instead of dealing with the issues at hand. When confronting the child about his or her misbehavior, the parent might blurt out, "Why did you act that way? If you had any sense, you wouldn't have done that." These words don't discipline the child or help the situation; they only make the child feel guilty and bad about himself. Recently, a lady told me how her grandmother used guilt trips to manipulate her mom. This grandmother would make the mom feel terrible for not visiting more often. For years, the mom kept trying to visit more frequently, but it was never enough. The grandmother always made her feel guilty. The more the grandmother tried to manipulate the mom into visiting, the less the mom wanted to visit. The result of the grandmother's manipulation was the exact opposite of what she wanted.

We do not need to put someone on a guilt trip or whine and complain to get what we want. Instead, we need to be adults and speak our minds openly. If you want help in some way, ask for it. Tell the person exactly what you need, but be willing to accept the answer, even if it is no. We will not always get our way, but the odds are better if we are forthright instead of manipulative.

Boldness and Organization

I tell people all the time that the spiritual and natural gifts we receive from God can often be used against us. For example, the gifts of faith and discernment can easily turn into presumption and judgment. Gifts like boldness and organization can be twisted into a form of control. Someone with these gifts might overpower others by making decisions for them and taking charge of their lives. The perversion of our gifts is another tactic that the enemy uses to steal, kill, and destroy who we are meant to be. Be aware of the enemy's tactics and don't allow him to cause your gifts to be used for the wrong purposes. God may have intended someone with the gifts of boldness and organization to direct the growth and development of a nonprofit ministry, but who wants to serve a controlling leader? Certainly not me.

Why We Control — Survival

I doubt anyone would be proud to call himself a controller, yet as I said, we all control to one degree or another. So why do we control?

I have found that a lot of people use control as a survival mechanism. I did that for years. I wanted some way to emerge unscathed from the bad things that kept happening to me. I started to think that if I kept all my ducks in a row, maybe bad things would not happen. I somehow felt that I had control over every outcome. Unfortunately, that was not true, and it caused great pain and confusion in my life. For example, I used to believe that if I prayed hard enough, I could keep things from falling apart. Inevitably, things fell apart, which left me discouraged and wondering why my prayers had not worked.

Over time, I realized that even prayer could be a form of control. Casting our burdens on the Lord and then taking them back is control. Often we pray in faith and then think that we can still somehow control things by worrying or mulling them over in our minds. The truth is that we are only wasting time and missing out on the good life God has for us. God is God, and his ways are higher than our ways (Isaiah 55:9). Our prayers are important, but we must be willing to allow him to do things his way. We settle for so much less than he has for us when we try to do things our way. God wants to do exceedingly above all that we dare ask, think, or imagine (Ephesians 3:20). When we allow control to become a stronghold within our lives, we are not able to receive all that God has for us.

If we feel we have to keep all of our ducks in a row for life to be okay, then we are deceived. Life is full of ducks getting out of line. Think about it. How often does everything in your life go according to plan? Usually, the minute you think you have lined up everything the way you want it, something changes. The truth be told, we are not in control nearly as much as we think we are.

Misconceptions

We tend to control others when we do not have a proper perspective of the control God has given us. Some people believe they do not have to be responsible since God is ultimately in control, while others believe that they are in control and God is not doing anything. Both extremes are dangerous. The truth is that God is in control more than we can even imagine; however, he is not in control of our choices. He gave us a free will, which gives us ultimate control of our lives, and we must be careful to use the control that God has given us correctly. The balance comes when we realize that we can control our choices but not other people.

Control is never the answer when it comes to someone else. Jesus calls us to love one another (John 13:34). To love someone is to allow them to be who they are. We can pray for each other and ask the Lord to change hearts when change is needed, but we are incapable of truly changing someone else's heart; only God can change hearts. Although control may bring temporary change, it never brings lasting change.

Fear

When my children were small, I would give them instructions as they left the house. I would tell them things such as *Do not talk in class, do not yell on the bus,* and so forth. I was trying to hold it all together—my children, my family, my home, and myself. In reality, my attempts at controlling my children made things worse. Every time I made a list of *do nots* for my oldest son, he would go out and do every one of them. He rebelled at my control. As my children got older, I was always instructing them to be careful when they were driving, to be home on time, and so on.

The truth is that I could not keep my kids out of trouble, and you cannot keep your kids out of trouble either. Our kids are the only ones who can keep themselves out of trouble. We can train and teach our children, but when they leave our sides, we must trust them to take responsibility for being who we have trained them to be. We cannot make them, or anyone else for that matter, do or not do something.

The control in my heart was obviously stemming from fear. I was afraid my children would go through horrible things, and I would suffer with them. Even good intentions, such as concern for our loved ones, do not justify controlling behavior. Anything we do to try to control others will lead to undesirable outcomes. When we control our children, we keep them from learning how to think for themselves and make good decisions. When we control our spouses, they become resentful. When we control our friends, they want nothing to do with us.

Losing control was my greatest fear. Remember, I was trying to keep all my ducks in a row. Insecurity was still the culprit behind the fear. I was placing my value in my role rather than in whom I was in Christ. I thought my children messing up and getting hurt would be a poor reflection on me as a mother, and I was concerned about what people would think of me.

Why We Allow Others to Control Us

The reason we allow others to control us is the same reason we try to control other people: insecurity. We can be insecure about who we are, what other people think about us, and our role in relationships. Many people are insecure on all three fronts.

When someone has little self-esteem, it is easy for them to be controlled. To esteem ourselves is simply to respect and love the person God made us to be. We are not meant to be jack-in-the-boxes, always pushed down by someone else; nor are we meant to be puppets on a string, maneuvered by others. If we do not have a true image of who we are, control will try to tell us who to be. Sometimes it seems easier to allow someone to control us instead of taking a chance on our own decisions.

It breaks my heart when I think about the people who have not only been changed but also crushed by someone else's control. These people have no idea who they are anymore. Let me assure you that although rediscovering our true identity and worth is not always easy, it certainly is possible.

One of my favorite movies is *The First Wives*

Club, a 1996 comedy featuring Goldie Hawn, Diane Keaton, and Bette Midler. The movie is about three college friends who are reunited when a fourth friend commits suicide. At the funeral, the three surviving women realize they are all facing the same reality that led to their friend's tragic death—unfaithful spouses and impending divorces. Divorce is an ugly thing, and it wounds everyone involved, but I remember watching that movie and being set free. What impressed me was the women's response at the end of the movie. The Bible says in John 8:32 that the truth sets us free. The truth was in the words of the song "You Don't Own Me," which they sang after confronting the issues of their failed relationships. This goes back to the principles I shared in the chapter on rejection. Others can own us only if we allow them to determine our value and worth.

I once counseled a woman who lived in constant fear that her husband would leave if she did not lose weight. This woman was genuinely trying to lose the weight. She was exercising, eating healthier food, and taking good care of herself while her husband tried to control her with anger, dominance, and unkind words. Every time he sabotaged her with this behavior, she would begin to do what she had always done when she disappointed him—eat. This went on for years until one day she decided she'd had enough. She resolved to lose the weight for herself.

From that day on, she remained focused on her plan for losing weight even when her husband put her down. Continuing to exercise, eat nutritiously, and take excellent care of herself, this woman made a conscious decision not to fall into her former, unhealthy eating patterns. As she started losing weight, she began to feel better about herself. At the same time, she learned that God loved her regardless of her dress size. The truth of God's unconditional love began to change her, and she developed self-respect. That may not be what you thought she needed to learn, but I assure you it was.

Any time we do things to keep other people from getting mad or upset with us, we are allowing them to control us. We should want to do better to be the best we can be for God. Like me, you may want to be a good wife, mother, friend, and employee, but you can't be if someone else is controlling you. The motive for your actions has to be love, not fear or insecurity.

To Please People

We can allow others to control us in an effort to please them. It is easy to manipulate people who live to please others. These people will do whatever you want them to and at any cost to keep you from being mad at them. The problem is that they cannot possibly keep everyone happy. It is only a matter of time before they eventually hurt one person to please another.

We are called to be God pleasers, not people pleasers (Galatians 1:10), and must learn to set healthy boundaries and do only what God is asking us to do. Not every need that comes your way is yours to meet; neither is every job you are asked to do your assignment. If we do what someone else asks us to only to keep from disappointing them, the motive for our action is not right. Moreover, while we are executing the task, we are often harboring dark feelings of resentment, which, in turn, hinders the job from being a true expression of the heart.

We will never be able to please everyone in our lives. Our job is to pray and do the things that are in our hearts. That does not mean that we do not have to go to work if we do not want to. God sometimes leads us to do things we don't necessarily want to do, but he always gives us the grace to do them. We should care more about being obedient to God than about trying to keep everyone else happy.

Pleasers can come across as peacekeepers. I used to control everything from when we would vacation to who would sit where on the trip. I took on a lot of false responsibility in order to keep the peace, and at the same time shirked my responsibility to be truthful and honest because I didn't want to take a stand.

While we should definitely pursue peace, this pursuit should not be at the expense of our own well-being. Sometimes in order to restore peace to our homes, we are going to have to confront difficult things in a spouse, child, or within ourselves. Pretending that the proverbial elephant is not in the room is not benefiting anyone, least of all ourselves. Sometimes peace comes with the sword of truth (my paraphrase). We must understand that there is a big difference between doing whatever we can to keep someone from being mad at us and doing what is right so that we are in a personal place of peace.

Misunderstood Submission

We can allow others to control us if we do not understand what it means to submit. If we think that submission is total compliance to another, we will do whatever anyone tells us to and exactly how he or she tells us to do it. To submit, however, means something slightly different.

Submission is yielding oneself to the authority of another. I believe in real submission because it's biblical; so is authority; someone has to lead. Every unit has to have a head who has been delegated the authority to lead or govern. The perfect illustration is Christ as the head of the church. In like fashion, God designed man to be the head in marriage. I have learned that it is easy to submit to someone in authority when you know he loves you and has your best interest at heart. Part of our journey toward freedom is learning to submit to the Lord and to the authority he has placed in our lives.

A widespread misunderstanding of submission has caused great pain over the years. Many men, especially Christian men, have used submission as a way to make their wives subservient. Can I say something? That is wrong. Wrong, wrong, wrong. Subservience implies that women are subordinate or inferior to men. That is simply not true. Women are just as important and valuable to God as men are, and God is very explicit when he tells us in Ephesians 5:21 (AMP), "Be subject to one another out of reverence for Christ (the Messiah, the Anointed One)." That is the essence of a healthy relationship and God knows it.

No one is created to live in another person's shadow. Every person on this planet matters deeply to God. Each and every one of us counts. We may not always get our way, but it is perfectly fine to have our own opinion; our opinions matter. Some people don't know this. Perhaps you have heard these words but never let them penetrate your heart. I encourage you to let the truth sink in. When you do, you will be less likely to allow another person to control you.

Effects of Control

No matter who does the controlling, whether the man or the woman, the effects are always negative. Harm always comes to the person being controlled, and often the relationship is destroyed. If control is fear based, which I believe it is, then it cannot bring life to someone; like the enemy, it can only steal, kill, and destroy. After years of hearing about and witnessing control firsthand, I began to recognize it by its effects. Control can cause us to become confused or foggy minded. If you have ever been controlled, you probably know what I am talking about but have never been able to put it into words. Being controlled will cause us to lose focus and clarity. When someone has been controlled for any length of time, they may find it hard to make decisions. To the victims, it actually makes sense to allow someone else to dictate their choices. If someone has regularly been making our decisions for us, then there is no room for us to become confident within our own decisions. Control causes us to doubt ourselves and what we are doing.

As stated earlier, when you are being controlled, it is as though you lose yourself. A young lady I know who was being controlled said it felt like a part of her authentic self was being taken away. That's exactly what control does; it chips away at our true identity.

The story about a woman named Jezebel in the Bible demonstrates the power of control. In the book of 1 Kings, Jezebel controlled her husband, Ahab, with anger and dominance. She kept him under her thumb and systematically treated him like a doormat despite the fact that he was the king. Ahab did not amount to much of a ruler. In fact, *wimp* would be a more appropriate title. Ahab allowed Jezebel to puppeteer mandates over which he should rightfully have reigned.

Ahab is not the only person Jezebel controlled. She also used intimidation to control the prophet Elijah. In 1 Kings 18:37–38, Elijah called down fire from heaven, proving to be the Lord's prophet. He put 450 prophets of Baal to shame and eventually to death, and when Jezebel heard this, she threatened him. Although this is singularly one of Elijah's most memorable feats, under the threat of Jezebel's intimidation, the prophet ran for his life, so in chapter 19, we find the great prophet hiding under a juniper tree. Can you imagine the sight of this mighty man of God seeking cover underneath the limbs of a tree that could barely shade him, much less protect him? The man who had boldly and successfully called down fire and prayed for rain was now begging God to take his life. Never underestimate the power of control!

After Elijah fell asleep in a state of self-pity (which, by the way, never does us any good), an angel of the Lord appeared to him. Twice the angel told Elijah to get up and eat because he had things to do. Finally, the Lord asked Elijah what he was doing there. What makes me laugh every time about this story is how Elijah exercised his faith for great miracles but not for his own protection. What's not so funny is how we, in our humanity, do the same thing. We tend to use our faith for the big things and forget that God wants to help us just as much with the little, day-to-day things in our lives.

Although Jezebel represents the extreme side of control, her story helps us to understand just how powerful and evil its effects can be. Jezebel's control continued until the prophet Elisha had Jehu deal with her in 2 Kings 9.

Control always results in discouragement and fear. How many times have you done something for the Lord that in your estimation was a remarkable deed, only to feel disheartened, worthless, or rejected afterward? Know that what you have experienced is not unusual. Discouragement and fear are two of the most effective tools that the enemy has used against God's people for years, and he's still using them against us. The enemy does not want us to win any battles in this war and will use whatever he can to defeat us.

Freedom from Control

We will never be free from the stronghold of control unless we recognize it, know the truth about it, and rely on God's power to deliver us. Be aware of the methods of control: anger, intimidation, dominance, possessiveness, and manipulation. Are you using them? Are others using them on you?

Watch for the effects of control. Is your mind foggy and clouded? Are you or is someone you know having a hard time making decisions or thinking on your own? Do you feel like you are losing yourself or notice the authenticity of someone you love slowly beginning to slip away?

Pray and ask the Lord to show you if you are being controlled or if you are controlling others. If you find that you are the controller, allow the Lord in his mercy to free you from that way of living. Ask for forgiveness from the Lord and from the people you have been controlling, and release them to be who they were created to be. Trust God to take care of you; he is willing and able.

If you are allowing others to control you, it is time to stand up and be counted. You are a valuable child of the Most High God, so do not agree with the lie that you are less than anyone else. You are just as important to God as the next person, and God needs you to know your worth and value so you can fulfill the destiny he has set before you.

You can get out from under someone else's control, but it will take determined work. Ask the Lord to cleanse you of any negative effects of control and then exercise your authority as a child of God, knowing that you have the authority in your own life to decide if you are going to allow someone to control you. In fact, Luke 10:19 says that you have been given all authority to trample on serpents and scorpions (the enemy). Get in the fight. Be fully engaged and refuse to wander in passivity. Read the Bible regularly and let the power in its words build up your inner man. Study the scriptures on your identity and become secure in who you are in Christ. Let God love you and trust him to meet every one of your needs including acceptance, approval, guidance, and protection.

Resist the urge to run out and push away everyone in your life who might be controlling. This may be your first inclination, but it is neither God's will nor his way. We are called to always walk in love. I can assure you that people who control usually do so from a place of hurt. They are trying to protect themselves and do not want to get hurt again. Do not be someone who causes more pain and rejection in their lives.

God created us for relationship. He never intended us to be controlled or to control others. Relationships don't work when one or the other controls. Think about it. If we pulled out a list of expectations for our spouse, the marriage would quickly be in trouble.

God is love, and as the embodiment of love, he gives each of us a free will, a choice to love or not to love, but he will not coerce us into subjection. God willingly chose and loves us regardless of the right and wrong choices we make. He continues to pursue us because he loves us so much, even when we choose to make stubborn and rebellious choices. His love always remains steady. Although God commands us to love our neighbor as ourselves, he still does not remove our ability to make an alternative choice. Love allows the other person to decide, so we see that we cannot love as God commands if we choose to control or allow others to control us.

God has given us responsibility for our own lives. We are not responsible for what others do; we are responsible only for what we do. If we do what we're not supposed to (controlling others), we won't be able to do what God has actually called us to. God knows what he put on the inside of us, and he has planned great works for each of us.

We can take proper responsibility for our lives by allowing the Lord to free and transform us into the people he created us to be. God is the only one who can help you overcome any and every stronghold that is currently holding you captive. You must turn to God and allow him to show you the way through the mire. Take your rightful place in life and let God be the one in control.

Instead of making decisions based on fear or what we think we ought to do, we need to be led by the Holy Spirit. He wants to guide and direct us. Jesus said in Matthew 11:30 (NIV), "For My yoke is easy and My burden is light." You will do more with God's anointing and power than you ever will on your own. The bottom line is that you do not always have to make things work out your way to keep those ducks in a row. Rather, let go and let God. God is faithful. You can be secure in him. God has the row and the ducks, but most importantly, God has you.

Dear precious Lord, I give you control of every part of my life. I trust you. Amen.

The Refuge of God

This chapter initially began as a private, journal-entry meditation between the Lord and myself and was affectionately entitled "A Letter to My Father." At the time, I was on a serious quest for an answer to a question that kept eluding me. While I had experienced some marked success in sustaining and maintaining the freedom Christ died and was raised to secure for me, I was acutely aware that there was still something missing, a hidden key that I needed to be able to articulate accurately to others so that they too might be able to intentionally experience sustained victory in every area of their lives as well.

My question? *How do I help people stay in a place of freedom once they've left the past behind?* So many believers today are better equipped to handle life's issues yet are still functioning out of a fractured heart that is riddled with hurt and brokenness. As we have all experienced, the storms of life will eventually return, and we need to be able to evaluate our lives to such a degree that we can rid ourselves of the old, worn-out methods and replace them with new and effective tools for living.

After asking the Lord how I might help people through the trials that might still come, he reminded me that we have a place to go in times of trouble (Psalm 46:1; Psalm 59:16). He is the answer. As Christians, we have someone to run to, someone who cares about the details of our lives. The Lord has many attributes, but the one I want to talk about is that he is our refuge, a strong tower that we can run to (Proverbs 18:10). And while he truly is our refuge, my search didn't stop there because now I wanted to know the how. I needed to understand how I would tell people to take refuge in God. How do we stay under the shadow of the Almighty? What does that look like in practical terms?

Psalm 91:1–2 (NIV): "He who dwells in the shelter of the Most High will rest in the shadow of the Almighty. I will say of the Lord, he is my refuge and my fortress, my God, in whom I trust." When we wake up in the morning, we need to speak to the Lord, thank him for another beautiful day, and consciously "say of the Lord, you are my refuge and my fortress, my God in whom I trust." All through the day, keep the line of communication open, discuss things with him, and when we are appreciative, thank him. If we do this continually, it will be just as easy when something difficult happens to tell him about that as well.

I don't know how to make it any simpler than this. You just *do* it! You make a conscious decision to take the refuge! (Please refer also to Psalm 18:30 and Psalm 25:20.) When things aren't going well, we have to make a choice to go to him. In faith, each of us has to go to him and find a place of protection and hope. We must have hope that God knows what we are going through and that he cares deeply for us. His promise to never leave us nor forsake us must be something we choose to believe in the process. We cannot, however, take refuge in him without knowing his love and character. Is it any wonder that the enemy works so hard at messing with our image of God? He does not want us to run to him for refuge. Too often, we have allowed our circumstances to lead us in the false belief that we cannot trust him.

When we intentionally embrace God as our refuge, we activate his protection that shields and insulates us from the effects of the storms. Sure, life happens, but as believers, we can and must choose to live a different way. Making God our refuge takes the sting out of what is going on. No one is exempt from going through tough times; however, we have someone who has offered himself as a place to run to in our time of need. The things that happen do not have to wound our souls so deeply as to etch pain permanently into our hearts.

In my immaturity, I used to believe that God should pluck us out of any bad thing that came our way. My inability to deal with pain kept me constantly on guard in an effort to avoid it. Since my understanding was grossly limited, I had no idea that the things that were hurting me did not have to have as much authority or permission to exist in my life as I had allowed. Like the drug addict who struggles to kick his habit but total freedom eludes him, I too kept holding onto old habits that I thought just might come in handy should pain resurface. The addict often begins his usage as a method to anesthetize his pain, but before he knows it, his plan to dull the pain becomes an addiction, a crutch he desperately leans upon when emotional trouble hits.

Leaning on God

Something came up recently that I know the enemy tried to wound me with. Someone close to me wrongly accused me of something. It wasn't that the person was mean to me, but the fact that she *believed* what she was accusing me of was a huge issue for me. This lady had made up her mind about what she thought, and that was that.

This attack was one that I was not sure how to combat. I prayed, warred, and did the usual things that I tell others to do; yet I felt like something was left undone. While discussing the matter with my sister, we joined in faith and prayed the prayer of agreement (Matthew 18:19). She said that while in prayer she discerned a huge brick wall had been erected to protect me. While a part of me was praying just to be delivered quickly from this unspeakable trial, the deepest part of me knew that I would not be delivered out of the trial, but rather I would find deliverance through the trial. The wall that my sister discerned was to serve as a shield while I persevered and allowed truth to win. As I went through the incident, it was totally different from how I had imagined it would be. With days leading to the climax, had you asked me to describe what this storm looked like, I could have told you how I thought the sequences would play out. I was very wrong. While the unspeakable did take place despite my diligent efforts to circumvent it, I still remained uniquely protected from the enemy inflicting hurt upon my soul.

The brick wall my sister had envisioned was God's refuge indeed. In my desperate cry to the Lord, even though I sought an end, he gave me his unrivaled protection. Sure, I had taken the accusation to the Lord, and I knew beyond a shadow of a doubt that I was innocent, so I could rest in the shadow of his wings, knowing I had a secret place to shelter during this terrible storm. In this place of security, I could choose to actively forgive the person maligning my character and in turn ask the Lord for boldness and love to deal with the issue. Needless to say, he answered every prayer.

I began to take comfort in the unwavering character of certain individuals in the Bible who went through terrible things, some even being put to death. I noticed that God had not delivered everyone out of their trials but instead had been a refuge through the difficulties. While we cannot control other peoples' actions toward us, we do not have to let what they do either define us or cause us to be wounded permanently.

Let's consider Mary, the mother of Jesus. Her entire adult life was shrouded with rumors and accusations that she had had a baby out of wedlock. Had Joseph, her fiancé, not received the visitation from the angel Gabriel regarding the truth of her pregnancy, he would have quietly put her away in secret. Thankfully, Joseph was open to the divine instruction he received and chose to believe the truth above a lie. In my own humanness, I wish that the angel had appeared to the religious leaders and to all the members of society at that time and informed them too of the divine seed that Mary carried within her womb, but that didn't happen. Years later, even the leading religious leaders of the day said with great disdain toward Jesus in John 8:41 (KJV), "We were not born of fornication." How would you and I respond to that type of accusation? Rather than spending his entire ministry defending himself against the merciless whispers surrounding his birth, Jesus simply stated the truth of who he was. He said, "Before Abraham was, I am" (John 8:58 KJV). In other words, Jesus's unwavering confidence and security in who his true Father was literally shattered the religious leaders' sacred cows. Those leaders greatly revered Abraham and considered themselves direct descendants of the great patriarch of their faith. Jesus simply pointed out to them this truth in laymen's terms: *I was there before Abraham was present, and I was there after he departed this earth, and I will also be here after you depart this earth because I am the Great I AM.* This really ruffled a lot of feathers because this young, thirty-year-old man was standing before his elders speaking with conviction regarding his deity. Even though it was not well received (they wanted to stone him for it), he stood firm in the truth.

Never once did Jesus ask to be vindicated, and as far as we know, neither did Mary, but both knew the truth. They knew who they were and whom they served. They allowed God to be their refuge.

Under His Wings

I recently began to ask the Lord about some things that had happened in my life that were painful. I wanted to better understand where he was during certain moments in my life. As I prayed about those incidents, I saw him pick me up with his wing and tuck me unto himself. As beautiful as that picture is, it was still not complete. I sat down to study and began to look up the words *wing* and *refuge.*

What I found was so exciting. Loving-kindness is mentioned almost always when God's wing or refuge is mentioned. The Lord began to show me that unless we understand the kindness of God's love, we will never run to him as our refuge. If we do not believe he is safe, we will not go to him for safety. Once we begin to allow our image of him to be healed, we can then draw close to him when we need a refuge.

Hebrews 13:5 in the Amplified Bible reads like this: "He (God) Himself has said, I will not in any way fail you nor give you up nor leave you without support. (I will) not, (I will) not, (I will) not in any degree leave you helpless nor forsake nor let (you) down (relax My hold on you)! (Assuredly not!)"

My eyes were further opened when I saw that we have a choice as to whether or not we will allow him to be that refuge. When we do not know that he is a safe place to run or when things around us seem like they are falling apart, we can miss the beauty of his refuge. There have been times in my life when the Lord just swooped me up in his wings and became my refuge without me even knowing it. However, as we mature in the Lord, we need to take responsibility to run to him for safety.

The perfect example of this is Christ Jesus. He was able to endure the heinous and arduous process of the cross because he knew first and foremost that God's unfailing love toward him would not leave him without hope. Being thus acquainted with his heart and irreproachable character, Christ could move into the unspeakable fray being confident of his Father's ultimate provision.

We can also consider Stephen's exemplary model of faith under trial as he went to his death with a smile on his face. Surely this was nothing short of a miracle (Acts 7:55). Because he was secure in who his true refuge was, he was able to die with dignity and assurance. Because of what Jesus did for us by dying on the cross and taking our sin and punishment, he made it possible for us to know God intimately and allow him to be our refuge. Therefore, the things that we go through can be endured with confidence and authority knowing we are not alone.

I know the pain in people's lives because I hear the stories. Betrayal, divorce, abuse, relationship problems, and rejection are meant from the enemy to wound our souls and cause us to be changed by the pain. God, however, has given us a place in him that keeps us from the depths of the pain that comes our way.

I believe wholeheartedly that we do not have to feel the pain of life as deeply as those without hope, nor should we allow our emotions to send us into a downward spiral of carnal behavior. There is no situation too dark that justifies allowing us to become overtaken and ruled by our emotions. Yes, in the face of grave difficulty, we can stand securely on the rock. We have something the world does not have and that is a safe place to run. He is the brick wall that keeps those things from going into our hearts as deeply as the enemy designed them to.

As I was studying this the other day, my cell phone rang. That may not be a big deal to you or I, but it is a huge deal to my dog. She gets so afraid when my cell phone rings. Although she is not allowed on the furniture, she proceeded to crawl onto the sofa and hide her head in the pillows, all sixty-one pounds of border collie. Fortunately for her, she did not need a real refuge, for had she needed protection, those pillows would not have done the trick. Most of us think that the things we hide behind somehow protect us from being seen by the enemy or the people in our lives who hurt us, but this premise is false.

We may be running to things other than a pillow, but nothing really works except God. There is nothing and no one else that can soften the blow or keep the thing from taking us out of the fight. When we make God our refuge, we take the stinger out of the sting. A wasp without a stinger may try to hurt its victim but will not accomplish it. Wouldn't it be nice to know the stinger has been removed even while the hurt is trying to sting you? Throughout the psalms, David talks about God being his refuge from his enemies. The only place of real protection is the refuge of our God.

Holding On

One of the strangest things I see the enemy has accomplished is making God's people soft. We are shattered over the bad things that happen in our lives, but we are also shattered over things that are not so important. The key to not being deeply wounded is to make sure we have dealt with the wounds from our pasts. If wounds are left unhealed, they will exaggerate any new disappointments or hurts that come our way. When we deal with the issues in our past, we then keep things in their proper perspective and subsequently have a better chance of making good choices. Simply stated, with every situation we get to decide just how far down the emotional hole we want to fall.

A friend of mine recently lost a job unjustly. This

lady had given her blood, sweat, and tears to her employer, working more hours than were asked of her just to get the job done well. Regrettably, she was poorly compensated and after a few years was axed based on the performance of her boss. I remember the phone call we had. She is a sensible person, but she became consumed not only with the injustice of what had happened but also with the fear of what she was going to do.

I love this lady because she and I have the gift of a rare covenant relationship. We might allow each other to go down in the pit about things, but just for a minute, and then come with a spiritual ladder of truth because we are coming out of that pit together. We can choose to deal with the situation righteously and refuse to be a victim to life.

Those hits that we take are meant as distractions. With God as our refuge, we don't have to be as easily distracted. We were created for God. If we have that as our big picture, then the smaller events in life which continue to harass us are not as successful at taking us off track with God. We are called and chosen to help build the kingdom of God. The people we know who have succeeded in life have done so because they have a vision of the bigger picture than only themselves. Life is so much more than *me!*

Every time we take an emotional hit, we have a choice. We can run to God as our refuge, knowing we can trust him to hold onto us, even if we are hurting and can't hold onto him. The other option is to fix our eyes and emotions on the hurt and lose our perspective. Perspective is a huge thing in this life. Ten people can see the same situation before them and have ten different perspectives based on their beliefs and ideals. In order to walk in the refuge of God, we must have his perspective. If we know him and his Word, we can take a step back from the pain and eventually see what we need to see.

The friend who lost her job is a great example because she was emotionally involved in the confusion of what happened, but after talking with her, she was able within just a day or so to take her eyes off herself and focus on God and his plans for her. As she began to take that perspective, she settled down and asked God what he had for her. She ran to him as her help! Within a week, she started a new job using all the skills learned in her previous employment. She received two weeks' severance by following through on what she felt God showed her to do and never missed a beat. Now, that's refuge!

God wants to be our refuge in times of any trouble, no matter what they are; he doesn't only hold onto us while we are going through those things, but he makes them not sting as badly and brings us out to a solid place. He is the only one who can do this. The only one! He is our rock and our refuge, a very present help in time of trouble. (Psalm 18:2) Whatever the trouble, he is there; he cares and he wants to see you through it without it piercing through you! He's that good! He is a refuge from anything that is purposed to pull us down. He is a refuge from shame (Psalm 71: 1), he is refuge against our foes (Psalm

61:3), and he is a refuge from the wicked (Proverbs 14:32), to name just a few.

When we learn how to go through the hard times of life, knowing we have a safe place to escape to, we can eliminate the cycles of pain and distraction. If every hurt or injustice were dealt with by trusting him to hold onto us, we would live the abundant life we all want so badly. Run to him! He is there! He is a very present help in times of trouble!

Dear precious Lord, thank you that I can run to you as my refuge in times of trouble.

Trust and Live!

I am currently sitting in a hotel room in Aberdeen, Scotland, as I pen these words. My accommodations happen to be situated in a beautiful town made of granite, and even though in the United States we've already passed the mark of spring, Scotland is still cloaked in a wintry blanket of cold. To date, I've been working on the book *Captive No More* for over a year, and still find it utterly ironic how difficult it is for me to express on paper what I love to teach on a continual basis.

The reason I mention my locale here in this land full of great legend is that I am in total awe of the intricate work the Lord has done in my life this last year. I don't even remotely remember asking him to do this work, nor do I recall any of my friends or colleagues praying specifically for this, but here, in Europe of all places, I find myself under the loving hands of the Father being carefully crafted on the potter's wheel. If you are anything like me, we sometimes feel like we've arrived at a place, as if there is no more work to be done in our lives, and at other times, we just settle for the status quo and do not really hope for more. I can, however, say with a resounding cheer that I am so glad that God is committed to our growth and that he doesn't leave us the way we are. In fact, nothing he has ever done has been mediocre! He is the God of the impossible, the one and only miracle worker in our lives. Give me a minute or two to adequately explain.

Living Life

My husband and I were headed out on a cruise on the fourth of March. Three days before we left for the trip, he asked me if I wanted to go with him to Scotland on the nineteenth of March. While that's not much time to plan and get leave from work, I did continue to pray about it all day to ensure I was not doing something without first bringing it to the Lord. Now, for some of you, traveling by plane may not be a big deal, but if you could walk in my shoes, you would discover how many wonderful opportunities I have allowed to slip past me due to fear. In fact, almost every time I have said no to something fun, fear was at the bottom of it. I started life off being anything but fearful, and now, years later, what

I realize is that God has truly restored that person. Determined to walk out my victory, I was finally able to void the familiar *no* and give my husband a yes to his offer at the end of the day.

I am sure that some of you can identify with how easily I had previously been able to place my life on hold. Regularly missing opportunities to grow, to expand, and to develop, I led a cloistered life full of fear and limitation. Like me, many of you have lost your model of trust.

I know that when trust is lost, fear enters. So many people have no model of trust. I hear many stories about people's lives and the things that have happened to cause them to build protective walls. What we have to understand is that when we live behind those walls, we are not truly living! These lives are ours for a moment, and we get to decide what we are going to do with them. How many of us have held back and not done things we should have because of fear, doubt, or mistrust?

Let me back up and tell you about the cruise first. Unlike me, my husband has not been a big fan of cruises, so you can imagine my surprise when he suggested we go on one. Of course, I had to seize this opportunity to take my ideal vacation and do so with my husband, and we had such a great time! We got onboard and began to look at the excursions offered on days of port. I had experienced them all, so I suggested that he choose an activity, and I would be happy to do whatever he wanted.

On the second day, he told me that we were going

to do something called a canopy tour in Jamaica. I had heard about that tour, and everyone who had been had raved about how much fun it was. A canopy tour is where you whip through a series of zip lines from several feet to several hundred feet through the tops of trees and over rivers, way up high in the trees.

We had so much fun. I probably sounded a bit like Tarzan as I yelled excitedly like a banshee through the turquoise-colored sky. I did not mind sounding crazy because it was so much fun racing down a zip line strapped in by just a harness and holding on tight. Years ago, I would never have done such a thing. It would have been much easier to talk myself out of it because for me these activities required trust, and I was badly lacking in that area.

The Monday after we got back from the cruise, I headed to the airport to meet my husband. I was a little nervous thinking about the fact that I was about to embark on the longest flight I had ever taken, but Scotland. Who says no to Scotland? We arrived in Aberdeen about twelve hours later, tired but excited to be there. Lance had been several times, but this was a first for me. He headed to work, and I got to rest. As I sat down to write this, I was overwhelmed by the enormity of the fact that I was there. I did it! I had flown to Scotland, done a zip line, and not only was I doing these things, but I was enjoying myself immensely. Here I was, having fun with all of these activities that were so unlike Tina, the fear-stricken, mistrusting woman who talked herself out of almost everything that was fun, eventful, or worth trying.

It's a shame how we allow fear to paralyze and hinder us from experiencing the good life Christ has in store for us.

Possibly you can relate to my former state. I cannot tell you how many times I've turned things down or skirted them because I did not want to find myself in a position where I might be afraid. When I look back over my life, I can see where I allowed my fear or fear of something bad happening to steal so much of my life. Although I know better than to stay in a place of regret, I am sorry for the fun things I've missed out on. Instead of regretting, I determined it was time to trust—not just anyone, but time to trust God.

God is completely worthy of our trust. We doubt him time and time again! Just like the children of Israel, our spiritual counterparts spoken of in holy Scripture, our human nature is to watch our heavenly Father do the most amazing miracles in and through our lives, become deeply moved, experience some level of gratitude, then after a short while, descend down the slippery slope of doubt, unbelief, and fear. Despite his unfailing goodness, we allow ourselves to become deceived into believing that we are alone, abandoned, and on our own.

Because of the confusion I had about God while growing up, it's been an incredible journey to learn to trust. For so many reasons, we may find our lives stuck in a place of not really knowing how to trust. Whether religion has taught us that God is mad at us or that we have to earn our way to him, we have thought we had reason to not trust. Throughout my healing, I've had to make choices about what to believe about God and what he really is like. Years ago, I concluded that God is good and that he is good all of the time. I choose to believe that no matter what happens; God is not the variable. I had to get there because I knew that without that in place, I would never make it in this walk.

I've heard so many extremes taught about God. The sermons that exclusively focused on the Old Testament aspects of God seemed to make him out to be an arbitrary tyrant who was always angry and disappointed with the human race. This description was difficult for me to embrace. Thus, I made a decision that if I was truly going to heal from my past, I had to stand strong on the goodness of God, no matter what came at me. When you are fighting for your freedom, you have to take a stand somewhere. No more being tossed to and fro by everyone else's opinions. I had to be okay with not having an answer for all of the *why* questions, such as, *Why do bad things happen to good people?*

The things that I have done, such as the zip line and the flight to Scotland, are examples of me trusting God to be in control of my life. Although God is in control, he has also given us the responsibility to pray, war, and believe. We have all been given the same rights to the tools that God has for us. I may not mind flying anymore. In fact, I enjoy it, but I'm certainly going to pray and ask for his protection and war and use my authority to keep the enemy away before I get on a plane. We have been given authority, but we have to take up that authority for it to be manifest in our lives. I can hand you a sword, but what you do with it is up to you. We have to learn to pray, believe, fight, stand, and trust! There is a combination that is necessary. Since we are in relationship with God, our part is to walk with him in such a way that we know our part in the circumstances we face. There are covenant promises given to us by the Lord, but if we do not know what they are, we may not draw from those promises. His promise of protection is a real one, but if we do not know that he promises to protect us, we may not stand in our rightful place of safety.

God is Good

You may be wondering how to reconcile all of what I'm saying. The bottom line is that God is good. He loves us more than we can ever imagine, and his heart toward us is good. His promises are yes and amen! The things that have happened in our lives that made us not trust him can be redeemed. I had to get to a place in God where I believed that I could trust him for my good. I decided to get on that zip line and have fun and get on a plane to Scotland because I know that my life is in his hands. The fear of death is so strong in so many of us, and it is at the root of why we struggle with all those other fears. I concluded that I am going to live life to the fullest, and if I die, I get to be with the Lord. There is nothing bad about that! I don't have a death wish; I want to be around to see my grandkids grow up and be in

their lives, but one thing I know is that I have committed my life to the Lord, and he is not going to let
anything pluck me out of his great hands.

Once we have a true revelation of God's love, we
can then trust and enter into a place of rest. We can
cease striving to be in control and place our lives in
his confident hands. Please know this: We are his,
and he loves us with an everlasting love. Whatever
things have happened to us that have been bad or
hurtful or even things we've done to derail our own
lives, he wants to redeem and give them back to us
better than they were before. That's the God we
serve. The hurts and disappointments we have faced,
God desires to restore and redeem them. He desires
to give you back all things that have been stolen from
you, including trust.

"There is no fear in love, but perfect love casts
out fear because fear involves punishment, and the
one who fears is not perfected in love" (1 John 4:18
NASB). If we really believe that our sins are forgiven
and that we have right standing with God in Christ,
then we do not have to fear punishment, either in
this life or after we go to be with the Lord. We can
know without a shadow of a doubt that we are going
to be with God at the end of our lives if we have chosen to accept the price paid for us by Jesus.

I believe that the best gift we can give God is our
lives. When we get to the end of our lives, what we
may have to answer for is what we did with the lives
God gave us. *Did I live or hide? Did I live and enjoy
or quit in fear?* It's never too late to decide to live!

I don't care how old you are; decide today that you are going to go out tomorrow and live! Really live! I want you to know that you can trust God. He cares about every detail of your lives and has you in the palm of his hand.

Unfortunately I trusted in my ability to hold it together and not God! When I was little, I remember taking control emotionally and decided I had to take care of us. I took emotional responsibility for my mom and myself. Understand that this was not some great heroic feat; this was pride at its worst. As a child, I was so hurt and angry over the things that were happening in my life that I judged God as being useless and me as being more capable of taking care of those I loved. That decision, however uneducated, tripped me up in most of my walk with the Lord.

God is Big

The things the Lord had to walk me through to find freedom are amazing to me. Little by little, in his great love, he whittled away at that pride and mistrust. God will draw us to truth for our freedom time and again, but we must go with him toward the truth for it to be effective in us. As I allowed him to break down those false beliefs and fears, I found a little more trust in my heart with each breakthrough.

I have always loved science. It was one of the few subjects in school that interested me and kept my attention. I love nature, animals, weather facts, and how this whole world stays together. I read a book last year called *I Am Not But I Know I AM*, by Louis Giglio, that broke through that wall of fear in a huge way.

As I read through the pages and was reminded of things such as a light year and how light travels, etc., I was shaken to the core of how big our God is. I sat on my patio and devoured the book. It's funny how any given book can affect us differently, but this one touched the very core of my problem. I wept before the Lord when I realized not just how big he is but how small I truly am. There was great freedom in that for me. In my heart, I got it. I had real understanding that this God I serve has the whole thing in his great and mighty hands. He not only flung the stars into space and knows each by name, but he also keeps the earth we live on rotating perfectly on its axis so that we don't all go flying off.

The bigger news is that he has us! He has you and I in his heart and in the palm of his hand. He is for us! He is committed to our good and loves us as his children. If he can hold the world in his hands and keep it running smoothly without our help, then I think he can keep me in an airplane. That is where I landed in my heart before getting on the plane to Scotland.

So many people have given up hope or let go of a dream because things didn't work out the way they expected. Unfortunately that can lead to us not trusting God, but God is never the problem. Maybe it's time to let go of that protective shell of mistrust. Let me encourage you to pick up those dreams again. It's time to dust off the areas in our hearts that have been disappointed, thereby causing us to give up hope and trust. God is faithful. He is for us; we've just gathered so many emotional protective devices that make it easier to be cynical.

There was a day in this process when the Lord spoke to my heart and showed me that I was cynical. I have to admit that was not what I expected to hear about myself. After years of walking with the Lord, I know when he speaks something like that to my heart that he is always right, so I decided to sit down and look at what he wanted to show me. As I dug into what I believed he was trying to get to me, I realized it was true. I had become cynical. I had grown sour, expecting to be disappointed. The sad thing is that it was nothing short of a protective guard I was using to keep myself from being hurt or disappointed. My expectation of disappointment kept me from hoping too much, thereby keeping my sights set low. Life is funny because we get what we expect.

As I repented for allowing myself to become cynical, I realized that it had been one of the things that kept me from enjoying the great things in my life, expecting to be disappointed set me up for more disappointment. I would pray for something and at the same time set my sights low. That's not faith or trust. God's love is so good that he wants to give you the desires of your heart. He wants to care for you and take care of things that concern you.

People may squelch our trust. Life may confuse us into believing that God cannot be trusted, but be assured, the God who loves us so richly can be trusted! I've wasted a whole lot of time trying to figure things out. Let me save you some trouble by telling you we are not going to figure God out or what he's doing. There are times when I have prayed, and warred, and stood, and still did not see what I was praying for come to pass. Did God let me down? Does that mean he cannot be trusted? No, he did not let me down, and he can be trusted. I believe that if we absolutely know his character and heart toward us, we can be fixed on his goodness, and when things don't work out our way, however disappointing, we can still stand and trust.

I was reading through some passages in Job 41 and meditating on what God is asking Job. He is explaining leviathan (crocodile) and how he cannot be tamed or beaten. In the natural, we understand and know what a crocodile is, but what I found interesting is that spiritually, it speaks of pride. In Job 41:34, God is asking this man to look at the fact that when we do not understand something, we have no problem questioning God. As it says in Job 38:1, without knowledge we question God, but we would not come against leviathan. It takes humility to trust in God, but our pride would have us demand understanding.

I want to help you understand that we only question God when we don't trust him. Because his mercy is new every day, he allows our questions, but I think he desires that we trust even when we don't understand. We have finite brains that cannot and will not be able to figure out God and his ways completely. We can, however, settle in our hearts that God is good all the time. Whatever you've been through, God will turn it for your good!

You can draw close! He is there and loves you more than you can imagine! It's time to take a leap of faith and trust that you can give up all of your self-protective ways, as well as give up trying to understand why things happen. When we settle once and for all that God is God and he is good, we set ourselves free to live.

Choose Life

Looking back over the wasted years in each of our lives can become quite sobering. If we have allowed the lies believed to cause rejection, fear, doubt, or mistrust, it's time to stop and choose the better way. We can take the tools in these chapters and apply them to help us overcome whatever strongholds have held us back. We must get in the fight to win. Whether you are just starting your walk with the Lord or are a seasoned Christian, there can be more to this life than simply surviving. It's time to live—really live.

If rejection has been the battle, choose to believe you are loved and accepted. If fear has been the battle, decide today that you were chosen by God, for God, and he has made you exactly as he wanted you. Decide today to trust and believe. That is the way we start tearing down the old and replacing it with the new and better way. Do not allow anything to keep you from living! We only get this one life, and

I believe we are training for reigning, so there is no more time to sit on the sidelines and watch life go by.

In conclusion, let me say that our number-one purpose in life is to love God, and our second is to love our neighbor as ourselves. With the strongholds dealt with, we can begin to take our eyes off ourselves and not only love God better, but we can also begin to show those in our lives what his love looks like. When we have our relationship with God right, we will also find it easier to be in right relationship with others.

We are told in John 13:35 that they will know we are Christians by our love. It's time to let the world see what that looks like, but that can only happen when we deal with our stuff so that it isn't sticking out for everyone to see.

May you find yourself living in God's marvelous love. It's a choice! Choose him!

Salvation Prayer

Heavenly Father, I humbly choose to believe that Jesus died on the cross for me. Jesus, I receive your forgiveness for my sins and ask you to come into my heart. Thank you that I now belong to you. Amen.

listen|imagine|view|experience

AUDIO BOOK DOWNLOAD INCLUDED WITH THIS BOOK!

In your hands you hold a complete digital entertainment package. In addition to the paper version, you receive a free download of the audio version of this book. Simply use the code listed below when visiting our website. Once downloaded to your computer, you can listen to the book through your computer's speakers, burn it to an audio CD or save the file to your portable music device (such as Apple's popular iPod) and listen on the go!

How to get your free audio book digital download:

1. Visit www.tatepublishing.com and click on the e|LIVE logo on the home page.
2. Enter the following coupon code:
   c95e-935b-aecc-b6d7-f2ca-67ae-d286-c5ec
3. Download the audio book from your e|LIVE digital locker and begin enjoying your new digital entertainment package today!